Maintaining the Foundations
A Study of I Timothy

French L. Arrington

Baker Book House
Grand Rapids, Michigan 49506

To my children
Lee, Athena, and Dan

Contents

Preface   7

Foreword   9

1   Maintaining the Foundations   11

2   Sound Doctrine   27
      1 Timothy 1:1–11

3   Our Vocation   43
      1 Timothy 1:12–20

4   Public Worship and Order   55
      1 Timothy 2

5   Standards for Leadership   73
      1 Timothy 3:1–13

6   The Character of the Church   91
      1 Timothy 3:14–16; 4

7   Proper Relationships   107
      1 Timothy 5:1–2, 17–25; 6:1–2

8   A Sense of Family in the Church   121
      1 Timothy 5:3–16

9   Fidelity to True Religion   137
      1 Timothy 6:3–10, 17–19

10   The Central Realities of the Faith   151
      1 Timothy 6:11–16, 20–21

Bibliography   166

Preface

T his book is an exposition of 1 Timothy. It is written with a conscious attempt to avoid the technical language of exegesis and to come to grips with the contemporary relevance of Paul's message to a fellow minister by the name of Timothy.

Maintaining the Foundations is meant to be a study book, and its aim is to help Christians in this present age of changes to hold to the basics of their faith. The issues dealt with in 1 Timothy have a remarkable relevance to the ongoing life of the church today.

The scriptural text should be read and studied along with this exposition. A number of commentaries have been prepared on the Pastoral Epistles. I hope that this study will encourage the readers to use other books and materials on these epistles.

I would like to express my gratitude to a number of my associates for their assistance in the preparation and the arrangement of the manuscript. Special thanks to Dr. Robert Fisher, who read the entire manuscript and whose suggestions regarding style and content have been very valuable. I am indebted to Mrs. Geraldine Brown for her patience and skill in preparing the typescript, and to Mr. Chris Thomas, a doctoral candidate in New Testament, for his support and perceptive comments. Also thanks to Mr. Bruce Tucker for assistance in research. I owe the greatest gratitude to Frances, my wife and best friend, who by encouragement and by reading the typescript has facilitated the composition.

French L. Arrington

Foreword

We live in a society that has reached a level of intellectual sophistication and scientific achievement unparalleled in history. Man stands amazed at his own accomplishments. Yet as he looks to what should be a bright and promising future, he has grave doubts about the soundness of the structure he has built for himself. The problems in the environment, the specter of economic calamity, the threat of nuclear holocaust—these things dog the steps of man and give him the uneasy feeling that his world could collapse at any moment.

The problems of society at large translate into feelings of anxiety, frustration, and insecurity for the individual. The shakier his world gets, the more intense his search for stability and security becomes. Thus the interest in "roots," and the push back to "basics." When the building is about to collapse, it is the foundation that must be checked.

Maintaining the Foundations is a book that speaks of things that are sound, and stable and secure. Its author, Dr. French Arrington, uses the message of the apostle Paul to his son in the Lord, Timothy, to assure an uncertain world that there is still a rock-solid foundation upon which to build one's life and future. In simple yet eloquent terms, Dr. Arrington brings the scriptural truths of 1 Timothy to bear upon current questions concerning vocation, worship, leadership, and family. He points out that the foundations of a successful and secure life can be maintained through fidelity to the Word of God.

French Arrington has become a master at translating the truths of God into practical application. *Maintaining the Foundations* beautifully demonstrates that ability. This is his third book in a series of topical commentaries. His two previous works, *Divine Order in the Church* (1 Corinthians) and *The Ministry of Reconciliation* (2 Corinthians), have received wide acclaim.

Dr. Arrington holds the Ph.D. in biblical languages from St. Louis University and the M.Div. and Th.M. in New Testament from Columbia Theological Seminary. He currently serves as chairman of the Department of Biblical Studies at the Church of God School of Theology in Cleveland, Tennessee.

> Robert E. Fisher
> Director of General Education

1

Maintaining the Foundations

Many currents and crosscurrents are present in the church today. Doctrinal winds are blowing in many directions. Heretical teachings masquerading as authentic Christianity are serious challenges to our faith. Christians need the ability to discriminate between truth and error. Change is occurring and will continue to occur. Change should be seen as a vital dimension to the ongoing life and health of the church. However, care must be taken that the foundations of the faith are not eroded. Nothing is more crucial to the life of the church than maintaining its biblical foundations.

Maintaining means preserving, conserving, caring for, keeping up, retaining. The foundations of the Christian faith encompass both doctrine and practice. The basis of faith and life in the first-century church was the teaching of "the apostles and prophets, with Christ Jesus himself as the chief cornerstone" (Eph. 2:20). "For no one can lay any foundation other than the one already laid, which is Jesus Christ" (1 Cor. 3:11).[1] So the foundations, strictly speaking, refer not only to Scripture but also to Jesus Christ, who is the heart and substance of Scripture.

---

1. All citations of Scripture are taken from the New International Version unless otherwise specified.

In every Christian fellowship a practical struggle goes on to maintain genuineness of Christian teaching. Counterfeits of Christian teaching are numerous and pose a threat to the very life of the church. The risk of divisiveness is always present in dealing with deviant teachings and practices, but it is a necessary risk worth taking. The apostle Paul was one who took this risk. God had entrusted to Paul's care the truth revealed in Jesus Christ. Paul's consuming concern was to preserve ". . . sound doctrine that conforms to the glorious gospel of the blessed God" (1 Tim. 1:10–11) and does not compromise the church's distinctiveness from the world.

What are known to us as the Pastoral Epistles (1, 2 Timothy and Titus) "depict the continuing life of the Church at the time when others were beginning to build upon its foundations. It had become necessary for the Church to establish itself in the world without compromising its distinctiveness from the world."[2] At that time the need of conservation was more urgent than that of innovation. Characteristically, then, much stress was placed on the diligent maintenance of the church's message. The fact that the integrity of the truth was crucial is suggested in expressions such as "the faith," "the commandment," "the teaching," "the charge," and "the deposit," all of which appear to refer to the whole body of Christian doctrine.[3]

When he wrote to Timothy, Paul's central concern, therefore, was the diligent conservation of the basic truth of the faith. Biblical truth requires more than mere intellectual assent to statements of doctrine. It is something by which all Christians are to live. Christian truth is for the heart as well as for the head and is to characterize all of the details of ordinary life. What is believed must be worked out in daily life, whether one is in the church or the world, in the bedroom or the kitchen, in the office or the factory, on the sidewalk or the highway. The cardinal truths of the gospel—the sovereign majesty of God (1 Tim. 1:17; 6:17), the incarnation of the Son of God and the magnitude of

2. Glenn W. Barker, William L. Lane, and J. Ramsey Michaels, *The New Testament Speaks*, p. 235.

3. Donald Guthrie, *The Pastoral Epistles and the Mind of Paul*, p. 23.

God's saving grace revealed in Him (1 Tim. 1:15), Christ's redemptive death that is adequate for all (2:6), the prospect of the final day of reckoning (1 Tim. 6:14), the ministry of the indwelling Holy Spirit (4:1; 2 Tim. 1:14; Titus 3:5), and noble virtues fostered by the gospel (1 Tim. 1:5–11; 6:11–12; 2 Tim. 1:13–14)—are the foundations for all Christian life and activity.

Maintaining the Foundations is an exposition of 1 Timothy, but since 1 and 2 Timothy are to be read and studied in tandem, frequent reference is made to the parallel material in 2 Timothy. To help us understand the message of 1 Timothy, we shall examine the background of the Pastorals and the issues raised by contemporary scholars in regard to these epistles.

I. The Pastoral Epistles

The Pastoral Epistles deal with the welfare of the church and the purity of the Christian faith and life. They provide instructions essential to the well-being of the church and thus gradually became known by the title *the Pastoral Epistles.* Paul Anton recognized that 1 and 2 Timothy and Titus addressed pastoral concerns. In 1726 he gave a series of famous lectures titled "The Pastoral Epistles." Since that time the letters have been known as the Pastoral Epistles.[4]

These letters are of particular value because the whole spiritual import of the gospel is brought to bear on the life and welfare of the church. Gross sins that would occur among carnal, immature believers receive little attention in these letters. The emphasis is on pastoral concerns that center not only in what Christians believe but also how they think and act. The gospel that Paul had received and had transmitted to Timothy and Titus was the church's standard for doctrinal soundness (1 Tim. 1:6–7; 4:6–7; 6:3–5), for attitudes toward state authorities (2:1–4; Titus 3:1–2), for right behavior (1 Tim. 1:8–11; 3:15), for relationships within the church (e.g., chapters 5 and 6), for the structure and worship of the church and for the qualifications

---

4. William Barclay, *The Letters to Timothy, Titus and Philemon,* p. 4.

of people within that structure (chapters 2, 3, and 5). Whatever issues the church faced were to be examined in light of the gospel.

II. The Situation of the Church

The Pastoral Epistles were written near the end of Paul's career, when the tendencies toward division were pronounced (1 Tim. 1:19f.; 2 Tim. 2:17; 3:8f.) and a clearer picture of the organization of the local church was beginning to emerge. Still in a developmental stage, the church, however, was entering a period of institutional stability.[5]

A. The Organization of the Church

The organization of the local church is somewhat unclear from the information in the major Pauline letters, but Acts reveals that Paul appointed elders in the churches he established among the Gentiles (Acts 14:23; cf. 20:17f.). Evidently the church at Jerusalem had developed the same structure (11:30). The apostle Paul refers to the leaders among the Thessalonians in his appeal "... to respect those who ... are over you in the Lord and who admonish you" (1 Thess. 5:12). The overseers and deacons provided leadership among the believers at Philippi (Phil. 1:1). The evangelists and pastor-teachers seem to have functioned as the leaders in the Ephesian church (Eph. 4:11).[6] Teaching and administration were among the gifts of the Spirit (1 Cor. 12:28).

From its beginning the church was not without leadership, but the Pastoral Epistles describe a fairly elaborate structure within the local church. The church was taking the first steps toward becoming a highly organized institution. Since competent leadership was vital to the life of the church, the personal quali-

---

5. Ralph P. Martin, *New Testament Foundations: A Guide for Christian Students*, vol. 2, p. 306.
6. The pastor-teachers were individuals who apparently were leaders in the local church with a twofold function of overseeing the flock and teaching.

fications and duties of the elders were set forth. Their function was threefold: ruling, preaching, and teaching (1 Tim. 5:17–22).[7] The personal qualities of spiritual excellence and duties of the overseer are also described in 1 Timothy 3:1–5.[8]

B. The Threat of Heretical Teachings

Apostolic Christianity was under attack in the churches for which Paul felt a responsibility. In the Pastoral Epistles the apostle combated what he regarded as false teaching and warned the churches against possible heretical influences. No one was to be allowed to teach "false doctrine." Such teaching was associated with speculation about myths and genealogies and led to vain discussions rather than to Christian growth (1 Tim. 1:3–4). At the heart of such false teaching seems to have been a misunderstanding of the law, which led to stress on knowledge and to a kind of pseudointellectualism that disregarded the moral claims of the gospel. Over against this Paul placed "sound doctrine," which conforms to the gospel (1:10–11).

Apparently the false teachers had come from within the church. They were already threatening to endanger the purity of the church's faith and morals. The profile of the false teachers was obvious. First, they wandered from the faith (1 Tim. 6:21). Second, they believed that they had already experienced the resurrection (2 Tim. 2:18). Denying, therefore, the resurrection of the body, they insisted on resurrection in a spiritual sense. They had already overcome the world, so they thought, and were living beyond suffering and the troubles of this life. Third, they rejected the belief in the fundamental goodness of creation. Inclined toward asceticism, they belittled marriage (Titus 2:4) and taught people to abstain from certain foods (1 Tim. 4:3). Over against the ascetic tendencies the duties of marriage are

---

7. What is stated in verse 17 indicates that all of the elders ruled, but all did not engage in preaching and teaching.

8. Whether the terms *overseer* (*episkopos*) and *elder* (*presbuteros*) describe the same person has been disputed. Titus 1:5f. speaks of both the elder and overseer and makes no distinction between them. This coincides with Acts 20:17, where Paul sent for the Ephesian elders (*presbuterous*) and urged them to guard the flock over which the Holy Spirit had made them overseers (*episkopous*).

stressed (Titus 2:4-5) and creation's goodness is vigorously stated: "For everything God created is good, and nothing is to be rejected if it is received with thanksgiving . . ." (1 Tim. 4:4). Fourth, they claimed knowledge (*gnōsis*, the word from which the term *gnosticism* is derived). Their interest was in speculative discussion—"foolish and stupid arguments" (2 Tim. 2:23) and myths and endless genealogies that promoted controversies (1 Tim. 1:4). What was godless chatter and was falsely called knowledge were to be avoided (6:20). No place was given to godless myths and old wives' tales (4:7).

Paul knew that grave dangers were present in the churches at Ephesus (1 Tim. 1:3-4) and Crete (Titus 1:5). The aim of the false teachers was to make significant modifications in the church's doctrine and life to accommodate the faith to false teachings. So in writing to two of his assistants, Timothy and Titus, Paul urged them to safeguard the truth against the dangerous threat of the gnostic teachers. The need for all Christians then and now is to uphold the truth in godly living and stand firmly in sound doctrine, knowing what is and what is not compatible with the gospel. Heresy always presents itself as a form of the truth and is, therefore, a greater danger to the faith than views that blatantly deny the claims of Christ. But the church that takes the gospel seriously must be prepared to speak out against error and if necessary to discipline those who profess to uphold truth while denying or contradicting it.[9] Frequently error masquerades as truth.

III. The Question of Authorship

Our discussion to this point has assumed that Paul wrote the Pastoral Epistles. Although each of these letters begins with the name of Paul, some critics contend that they come from a later period and are not part of Paul's correspondence. According to this view, whoever wrote them wrote under Paul's name and

---

9. I. Howard Marshall, "Orthodoxy and Heresy in Earlier Christianity," *Themelios* 2 (1976): 14.

spoke as he thought Paul would speak to conditions in the church.[10] The arguments against Pauline authorship are many.

1. The historical setting. With the exception of the Pastorals, the material in all of Paul's letters tallies with that in the Book of Acts. However, the Pastoral Epistles ascribe to the great apostle activities that are not described to us in Acts. Paul seems to have had an extensive ministry in Crete (Titus 1:5) and planned to spend the winter in Nicopolis (3:12), but Acts makes no mention of his mission to Crete or of the particular winter. According to Acts 20:1–3, Paul made two trips into Macedonia, but on neither occasion are we told that Timothy was left behind at Ephesus (cf. 19:22). However, 1 Timothy 1:3 indicates that apparently at a later time Paul had left Timothy in Ephesus to deal with teachers of false doctrines. Aware of the difficulty of fitting Paul's ministry as it is described in the Pastorals into the narrative of Acts, E. Earle Ellis says,

> The implication in II Tim. (iv. 13, 20) that Paul recently had been in the East does not fit the framework of Acts (xxi. 29; xxiv. 27; xxviii. 30). It is not impossible to place I Tim. and Titus in the period following Paul's final departure from Ephesus (Acts xx. 1). . . . But the traditional post-Acts dating of all three letters is more probable, and most critical questions have been addressed to this view.[11]

Admittedly it is difficult, if not impossible, to fit the picture of Paul in the Pastorals into the framework of Acts. Does this mean that the Pauline authorship of these letters is no longer credible? Likely the Pastorals describe conditions that belong to a period later than the history of Acts. Absent from Acts is any hint that Paul died at the close of the book or that he was released from house arrest in Rome. The testimony of Clement, a late second-century writer, is that Paul was released and went to Spain after

---

10. A popular view has been to deny the Pauline authorship of the Pastoral Epistles but to concede that Paul did have something to do with them. That is, sections in the letters are considered to be based on notes or fragments of genuine Pauline epistles. See P. N. Harrison, who, in *The Problem of the Pastoral Epistles,* first identified five Pauline fragments in the Pastorals, but subsequently reduced the number to three. Compare Donald Guthrie, *New Testament Introduction,* p. 590.

11. *Paul and His Recent Interpreters,* p. 52.

his first Roman imprisonment (1 Clement 5:5–7). Charges against Paul must not have stood up in a Roman court or were not taken seriously enough to bring him to trial.

The apostle seems to have been set free from the Roman house arrest of two years in A.D. 63 and visited Spain[12] and the Aegean area before his rearrest and death in A.D. 67.[13] This assumes a second Roman imprisonment, and thus between his release from house arrest in Rome and his rearrest he had a ministry for two or three years. Such a reconstruction allows Paul to have written the Pastorals in the closing years of his life. And, too, these letters record many of Paul's movements in those years when we are told he visited Ephesus (1 Tim. 1:3), Crete, Nicopolis (Titus 1:5; 3:12), Corinth, Miletus, and Troas and was finally taken to Rome (2 Tim. 4:20; 4:13; 1:17).

2. *The vocabulary and style.* A relatively large number of words appear in the Pastorals that do not occur elsewhere in the Pauline letters.[14] Because Paul did have a characteristic style and vocabulary, some critics think it is impossible to ascribe the Pastorals to him. It is well to be aware that circumstances and subject matter exert a powerful influence on both vocabulary and style. The rise of fresh problems could have been responsible for most of the new words. And, furthermore, the Pastorals seem to have been written at a stage in Paul's life quite distinct from the period reflected in Philippians, Colossians, and Ephesians.

While a number of words and phrases characteristic of Paul are missing from the Pastorals, Guthrie makes two penetrating observations:

> The first is that the subject-matter and the purpose of writing appear to have a direct bearing on the vocabulary; and the second is that no

---

12. At the time he wrote Romans 15, missionary work in Spain was part of Paul's future plans.

13. Ellis, *Paul and His Recent Interpreters*, p. 15.

14. Appearing in the Pastorals are 306 words that are not found in the other letters of Paul. See Bruce M. Metzger, "A Reconsideration of Certain Arguments Against the Pauline Authorship of the Pastoral Epistles," *The Expository Times* 70 (1958): 91–94, for an evaluation of statistical analysis in determining the authorship of the Pastorals.

amount of mathematical calculation could have predicted the working vocabulary of one group of writings by means of the other. But does anyone seriously doubt that one mind was capable of such remarkable variation? Rather we would suggest that the great variation in vocabulary in the case of Cicero is a measure of the greatness of his mind.[15]

Difference of vocabulary and style does not prove difference of authorship. As an example, E. J. Goodspeed has written technical New Testament works, yet translated the New Testament into popular language. The linguistic peculiarities of the Pastorals should not be divorced from the subject matter and the purpose. A major concern in these letters is to combat the gnostic teachers. Could Paul not use the slogans and language of his opponents against them, as he does in 1 Corinthians and Colossians? This certainly is a possibility. It seems that the three Pastoral Epistles can reasonably be understood to be genuine Pauline letters.

3. *The organization of the church.* According to this argument, the church, as it is portrayed in the Pastorals, is too complex for Paul's time. The church does appear to have been more organized than that pictured in the Book of Acts. Reference is made to elders, overseers, deacons, and an order of widows. The terms *elders* and *overseers* appear to be used interchangeably (Acts 20:17, 28; Titus 1:5, 7), but in the first century elders were nothing new. They assisted Moses in the government of the Israelites (Num. 11:16, 24). Too, on Paul's first missionary journey, he appointed elders in every church (Acts 14:23).

A number of New Testament scholars believe that the office of deacon had its beginning in Acts 6 when seven men were chosen to care for the widows and other poor people. The Epistle to the Philippians opens with a reference to deacons. Nothing is mentioned elsewhere in the New Testament about the order of widows, but in light of such passages as Acts 6:1; 9:39, 41 it is highly possible that the order emerged in the church in the middle of the first century.

---

15. *The Pastoral Epistles and the Mind of Paul,* p. 8.

The organization of the church and the function of its leaders, as the Pastorals portray them, must not be thought of as belonging to a period later than that of Paul.

4. The doctrinal viewpoint. Characteristic Pauline doctrines, we are told, are passed over in the Pastorals. Does the evidence lend support to this view? The typical Pauline doctrine of Christ's saving grace is found in the Pastorals. "Having been justified by his grace, we might become heirs having the hope of eternal life" (Titus 3:7). God's whole plan of salvation is put into effect by His grace (Titus 2:11). As in his other letters, Paul is conscious of his personal debt to the superabundance of divine grace (1 Tim. 1:14). God's saving activity is due to His own eternal purpose and grace. This grace is not earned but, as is so characteristic of Paul's teaching, it ". . . was given to us in Christ Jesus before the beginning of time" and "has now been revealed through the appearing of our Savior, Christ Jesus . . ." (2 Tim. 1:9–10). Though prominence is given to the sovereign character of grace, Timothy is urged to "be strong in the grace that is in Christ Jesus" (2:1), as Paul also stresses man's appropriation of divine grace.

The characteristic Pauline emphasis on the power and witness of the Holy Spirit, so some scholars contend, is missing in the Pastorals. While the references to the Holy Spirit are few, an examination of these epistles fails to support this contention. The emphasis of 2 Timothy 1:14 on the indwelling presence of the Holy Spirit is in full accord with Pauline doctrine, as is the Spirit's disclosure of apostasy in the last days (1 Tim. 4:1; cf. Eph. 3:5). According to Titus 3:5, spiritual renewal is by the Holy Spirit. Such a teaching also must be agreeable with Paul's thought. However, when Paul speaks of the process of renewal, he ordinarily makes no direct reference to the Spirit (Rom. 12:2; 2 Cor. 4:16; Col. 3:10). No doubt Paul himself would endorse the Spirit's work as essential to the renewing experience of the believer. Also there is an obvious similarity between Titus 3:6, the Holy Spirit "whom he [God] poured out on us generously . . ." and Romans 5:5, ". . . God has poured out his love into our hearts by the Holy Spirit. . . ."

The doctrine of the Holy Spirit in the Pastorals is in complete agreement with Pauline teaching. Of course references to the Holy Spirit in these epistles are not many, but this provides no valid reason for denying Pauline authorship. Colossians, an epistle generally accepted as written by Paul, mentions the Holy Spirit once only (1:8), and He is not mentioned at all in Philemon.

5. *The type of false teaching.* The point urged against Pauline authorship is that the heresy envisaged in the Pastorals was a second-century development in the church. Some critics have insisted that the false teaching denounced in the Pastorals was a mature kind of gnosticism present in the second century and thus these letters must be dated later than Paul's day. Some of the characteristic elements of gnosticism are that the world was not created by the God of the Old and New Testament but by an inferior deity; the material world, including the human body, is essentially evil and only spirit is good; knowledge based on revelation of profound secrets rather than on the intellect is stressed; and ethics range from extreme asceticism to unabashed libertinism.[16]

The false teachings disclaimed in the Pastorals are similar to gnosticism but do not have the fully developed character of second-century teachings. There are warnings against "myths and endless genealogies" (1 Tim. 1:4), against *gnōsis* that "is falsely called knowledge" (6:20), and against controversies and arguments (6:4; 2 Tim. 2:23; Titus 3:9). We may infer that the false teachers advocated spiritualism—the resurrection had already taken place (2 Tim. 2:18); asceticism—marriage and certain foods were to be avoided (1 Tim. 4:3); and legalism— commandments that turned men from the truth and gave rise to the ascetic view that "nothing is pure" (Titus 1:14-15).

Apparently what is repudiated in the Pastoral Epistles is not mature gnosticism, but embryonic gnosticism. Rather than dealing with full-grown gnosticism, these letters deal with what might be described as the seeds of gnosticism—beliefs and

---

16. See Edwin Yamauchi, *Pre-Christian Gnosticism*, pp. 13–28, for a discussion of the nature of and a more comprehensive list of the characteristics common to gnosticism. See also French L. Arrington, *Paul's Aeon Theology in I Corinthians*, pp. 181–187.

practices that had begun to germinate in the first century but did not come to full fruition until a later time.[17]

The false teaching that prompted Paul to write the Pastorals represents the beginning stages of gnosticism. The basic ideas that molded together practices and teachings contrary to Christian life and doctrine were already extant, even in Paul's time. When this and the historical circumstances are taken into consideration, a strong case can be made for accepting these letters as Pauline.

Arguments proposed against the Pauline authorship can be readily answered and good reasons given for understanding that the Pastorals came from Paul's hand.

IV. The Pastorals and Paul's Activities

Admittedly, the missionary activities of the apostle mentioned in the Pastorals do not seem to fit into the period of Paul's life up to his arrival in Rome. The Book of Acts ends by telling us that Paul spent two years under house arrest at Rome and that he preached the gospel without hindrance. But there is no word in Acts about the outcome of the captivity. It seems reasonable to suppose that the apostle was released after two years of imprisonment (A.D. 63). In fact he was expecting to be released. When he wrote to the Philippian believers from a Roman prison, he expressed hope of sending Timothy to them shortly; but he added, "I am confident in the Lord that I myself will come soon" (Phil. 2:24). Returning the runaway slave Onesimus to Philemon, Paul wrote, "Prepare a guest room for me, because I hope to be restored to you in answer to your prayers" (Philem. 22). Upon release he naturally would resume his missionary efforts. Timothy, Titus, Luke, and perhaps others accompanied him. This would allow for a second period of activity, even a visit to Spain. A scheme for the dating of this period of ministry is:

---

17. As some scholars have suggested, it may be more appropriate to reserve the term *gnosticism* for the second-century heresy and use the term *gnōsis* to speak of the beginning stages of the heresy described in the Pastorals, Colossians, 1 John, and other Scriptures.

release from the first Roman imprisonment—A.D. 63

ministry to Spain and the Aegean area—A.D. 63–66

execution in Rome—A.D. 67

A look at each of the Pastoral Epistles will help us to sketch the last years of Paul's ministry.

A. 1 Timothy

As we have assumed, Paul was released after two years in Rome. During what has been called the second missionary period he wrote both 1 Timothy and Titus.

On his last journey to Jerusalem the apostle gave a farewell to the Ephesian elders. At that time he did not expect to be able to return to Ephesus (Acts 20:25, 37–38). However, when he was released from Roman imprisonment, he probably visited Spain as he desired (Rom. 15:24, 28) and then returned to the eastern Mediterranean area. Among the places that he and his co-workers stopped was Ephesus. There the apostle urged Timothy to stay in the city while he continued on into Macedonia (1 Tim. 1:3). His intent was to rejoin Timothy at an early date (1 Tim. 3:14; 4:13), but he knew that in the Ephesian church were self-styled teachers who were spreading false doctrines and that he could be detained from rejoining his son in the faith. So he wrote to Timothy encouraging him to fulfill his duties as a minister: "... I am writing you these instructions so that, if I am delayed, you will know how people ought to conduct themselves in God's household, which is the church of the living God, the pillar and foundation of the truth" (3:14–15; cf. 4:13). 1 Timothy was written from Macedonia about A.D. 64.

B. Titus

Like Timothy, Titus was Paul's convert and coworker. He traveled with Paul on the latter's third missionary journey (2 Cor. 2:12–13; 7:5–16), but Scripture is silent as to whether he was with Paul during the first Roman imprisonment. After release from captivity Paul visited Crete with Titus.

There were Cretans present in Jerusalem to hear Peter's

sermon on the day of Pentecost (Acts 2:11). If they were converted and later returned to their home, it is probable that they organized a church.

The apostle Paul stopped at Crete on his voyage to Rome (Acts 27:7–21). Before the final Roman imprisonment he must have returned to the island to evangelize the residents. Apparently churches were planted in the major cities. Titus was left in charge of the work on the island (Titus 1:5). Later writing of his future plans, Paul expressed his desire to spend the winter ahead in Nicopolis in northwest Greece. So he asked Titus to meet him there as soon as Paul sent Artemas or Tychicus to replace him in Crete (3:12). There is no way of knowing whether Titus did that, but he was with Paul for the second Roman imprisonment. In Paul's last book mention is made that Titus had been dispatched to Dalmatia (2 Tim. 4:10). The letter that bears the name of Titus probably was written by Paul soon after 1 Timothy (A.D. 64). It must have been sent to Titus while he was still in Crete to instruct him in the performance of his task.

C. 2 Timothy

The atmosphere and scene change in Paul's last letter. Paul, previously free and without any premonition of danger, now is in Rome as a prisoner for a second time. Within about three years of his release from Roman captivity, he was arrested again. No one really knows why, and the place of his arrest is unknown. Some have suggested that Nero blamed the Christians for burning Rome. The Christians might have been convenient scapegoats, since they taught that the earth would be purged by fire (2 Peter 3:10–13). Nero, knowing that Paul was a leader of the new religion, had him arrested for the last time.

But others are convinced that Alexander "the metalworker"[18] fiercely attacked the apostle's message and brought criminal charges against him (2 Tim. 4:14). The occasion could have been when all the Christians in the province of Asia, including

---

18. This Alexander is likely not the same one mentioned elsewhere (Acts 19:33; 1 Tim. 1:20).

Phygelus and Hermogenes, abandoned him (2 Tim. 1:15). It is very probable that Paul was arrested in Troas. If Alexander's charges led to a quick seizure at Troas, this would explain why he left behind his personal possessions: cloak, scrolls, and parchments (2 Tim. 4:12). At Paul's trial in Rome, Alexander could have been a witness for the prosecution (4:14). The apostle refers to his "first defense," which must have been a preliminary investigation before his formal trial. Conspicuously absent were those believers who could have vindicated him. "No one," writes the apostle, "came to my support, but everyone deserted me" (4:16).

As a prisoner in desperate straits, Paul wrote 2 Timothy from a Roman jail shortly before his execution (A.D. 67). His second imprisonment must have been like snatches of a nightmare. Onesiphorus, unashamed of Paul's chains, had sought out the imprisoned apostle and had comforted him (1:16–18). The final chapter of 2 Timothy gives us a glimpse of the apostle's ministry as it drew to a close. Demas had deserted him. He would have enjoyed the presence and comfort of his closest associates. Dedicated as he was to the work of the gospel, he had sent Crescens to Galatia, Titus to Dalmatia, and Tychicus to Ephesus. Only Luke was still with him. In circumstances of loneliness and suffering his confidence for the future remained firm. His mind was on eternal realities when he triumphantly wrote, "The Lord will rescue me from every evil attack and will bring me safely to his heavenly kingdom" (4:18).

V. The Main Purpose of the Pastorals

Counterfeit teachings were present in the church. Beliefs and practices contrary to the Christian faith were creating serious problems. Heresy had already made inroads into the church at Ephesus where the young man Timothy was in charge (1 Tim. 1:3). Likewise the churches in Crete for which Titus was responsible were in deep trouble because of flagrantly heretical teachers (Titus 1:5f.).

The apostle Paul's chief concern in the letters to his assistants, Timothy and Titus, was to warn against corrupt teachings that were creating an identity crisis for many Christians and to give guidance for the administration of local churches. Underlying Paul's assessment of the difficulties in the churches was his burden to maintain the foundations of the faith.

Our situation in the church is essentially no different from that of Paul's day. There are still counterfeits and perversions of the truth. Compromise of the Word of God and accommodation of our lifestyles to practices contrary to the truth are common in the church today. The apostle Paul's prescription, the maintenance of the truth, remains sound because the power of the Word of God is for all ages. The Word of God in its full integrity can give continuity to the church's faith and life in the midst of all its changes and processes.

Sound Doctrine

(1:1–11)

T he gospel of God's grace was what the apostle Paul had faithfully preached wherever he ministered, and it was this message that he urged Timothy to proclaim and guard with all of his might. A strong appeal for sound doctrine was made by the great apostle. The proper boundaries of Christian belief had been established in the apostolic message—the word from God that spoke of what God did in Christ for all those who believe.

Ministry may be adjusted to changing realities without abandoning the unchanging reality of the truth. The community of believers stands under the unchanging gospel and is held accountable for it. As Paul explained to Timothy, the maintenance of the indissoluble integrity of the gospel is crucial to the life and the work of the church. But Timothy at Ephesus was faced with grave difficulties. As had been foretold, false teachers, who were attacking the faith and seeking to wreck the church, had arisen in the Ephesian church (Acts 20:17–31). These teachers were a real threat to the truth of the gospel and the moral life of Christians. The apostle to the Gentiles sent instructions for guidance and issued a call for utter loyalty to sound doctrine.

I. A Greeting (1:1-2)

Paul, the writer, was "an apostle of Christ Jesus." This was more than a letter from one friend to another. It was authoritative guidance for the church. Timothy was certainly not ignorant of Paul's apostolic authority. The reference to his authority was designed to strengthen Timothy's hand against the false teachers and to give more weight to the instructions of this letter.

A. The Divine Commission (1:1)

Paul's own commission was not by a church but "by the command of God our Savior and of Christ Jesus our hope." By the order of God Himself, he had been called to ministry. His orders came from one greater than himself. His calling was from the King of Kings. His authority was a God-given authority and rested in God our Savior and Christ our hope.

It is proper for God to be spoken of as Savior. While it was more common for Paul to speak of Christ as Savior, the title is apt for God the Father. As is made clear in other Pauline letters, the heavenly Father is the ultimate source of salvation. "You will be saved—and that by God" (Phil. 1:28). "God was pleased through the foolishness of what was preached to save those who believe" (1 Cor. 1:21). God "... did not spare his own Son, but gave him up for us all" (Rom. 8:32).

God gave His Son. The logical and fitting truth is that God is Savior, but a truth of equal weight is that Christ is our hope. He is the foundation of hope and expectation. Blessed is life now with Christ in the present world, but the fullness of salvation is yet to come. The One who "appeared in a body" and "was taken up in glory" is our hope (1 Tim. 3:16). As Paul says, "... Christ in you, the hope of glory" (Col. 1:27). With eager expectation we wait for the second appearing of Christ.

The basis of our hope is the saving power of God, disclosed in the death and resurrection of Christ. Our authority for ministry, like that of Paul, is from God our Savior and Christ our hope.

B. The Address to a Spiritual Son (1:2a)

Timothy was Paul's spiritual son. It was probably at Lystra, on the first missionary journey, that Paul won him to Christ. The relationship had deepened because of their partnership in the gospel. With personal affection and endearment Paul described Timothy as "my true son in the faith." His friend Timothy had experienced a spiritual rebirth. He was no pseudo-Christian or nominal believer. He had a sound understanding of the Christian faith and his loyalty was to the Savior.

Paul and Timothy were comrades in the faith. There are many relationships into which we may enter—business, social, educational—but none can satisfy the need for community and spiritual fellowship as does fellowship in the faith. This is the most invigorating and fulfilling kind of fellowship.

C. A Pronouncement of Blessings (1:2b)

As was customary, Paul began his letter with blessings. The blessings that he pronounced on his convert Timothy are "from God the Father and Christ Jesus our Lord."

The apostle spoke of the unlimited goodness of God by employing three terms: grace, mercy, and peace. Grace (*charis*) is an umbrella term and encompasses all that God has done to redeem man. Grace is God's unearned, undeserved favor, which through Christ reconciles man to God and to his fellow man. God is eager and ready to bestow His grace. It is a powerful reality, blotting out the sins and the guilt of the unsaved. It covers a multitude of sins and issues in eternal life.

Man needs grace and pardon for the past. He also needs mercy (*eleos*) for the present and the future. Mercy is God's loving-kindness and warm affection toward those who are perplexed and threatened by life's situations. There is the special need of God's tender concern in the experiences of distress, in the times of misery, and in the midst of perplexing and frustrating problems.

God's saving grace transforms human life, and His compassionate kindness provides strength for the unfortunate. Peace (*eirēnē*), accompanying God's loving purpose, is manifested in His pardoning grace and in His unlimited mercy to those who have fallen on hard times. The triumphal reality of grace and

29

the comforting strength of mercy result in peace and tranquillity. Peace is only through the grace and mercy of God.

II. An Admonition (1:3-7)

At this point the apostle turned to the business at hand. At Ephesus there were teachers of the law, that is, of legalism. They were disseminating the wrong doctrine about humanity's relation to the law of God as revealed through Moses. Timothy was tempted to leave the city. There was strong resistance to the truth in the Ephesian church, but Paul challenged his young friend to stay and confront the situation with sound doctrine.

A. Stay Where You Are (1:3a)

Timothy's presence was desirable so that he could continue to fight for the truth. The strong admonition suggests that there was a reluctance on his part to remain in Ephesus. Perhaps he preferred to travel with Paul or shrank from the task because of his timid nature. However, the truth needed to be defended. This was the reason Paul left his friend in Ephesus when the apostle went into Macedonia. Timothy's duty was near at hand, but a far-off place like Macedonia might have had more appeal to him. At that time his obligation was at Ephesus. That was where he was needed.

At times God's command may clearly be to move on to a new field of ministry. But we do well to remember that there are times when God's directive is "stay where you are."

B. Teach No Other Faith (1:3b)

The need for Timothy to stay in Ephesus was so that he might continue to fight for the truth. "Certain men" were teaching false doctrines. In verse 7 they are described as "teachers of the law." Timothy was to deal with these self-styled experts in the Mosaic law. Their intent was to force certain trivialities of Judaism on this church that was made up mostly of Gentiles.

As far as Paul was concerned, the result was disastrous. He

described the false doctrines of the teachers as myths.[1] Those who were polluting the gospel occupied their minds with myths or fables. In light of Titus 1:14 these were likely "Jewish myths," which consisted of Jewish stories or allegorical interpretations of the law. Fictitious interpretations that corrupt the truth attract some people. Just as Paul predicted, "...they will gather around them a great number of teachers to say what their itching ears want to hear. They will turn their ears away from the truth and turn aside to myths" (2 Tim. 4:3–4).

The false teachers also emphasized genealogies. The gospel could have gotten lost in ridiculous genealogies. Allegorizing of Old Testament genealogies could be endless because the only restriction on the interpreter is his own imagination and ingenious ideas. The spinning of yarns and subjective interpretations offer the Christian no insight into God's Word. Are the excesses of some Christian typologists in their treatment of the Old Testament not another form of the same problem? Those people find all kinds of hidden meanings in the Scriptures and propose interpretations that only cloud the truth. While the world is perishing in its need of the gospel, they spend their time and energy on vain speculations and extravagant interpretations. Their unrestrained fancy and inventions are fruitless, promoting "controversies rather than God's work" and forcing Scripture itself into a use contrary to God's intention.

C. Reprove Teachers of Novel Doctrines (1:6–7)

Myths and fables led people away from God's truth. Timothy was to put an end to the vain speculations of the false teachers. He was a man of authority, and Paul expected him to take a firm stand for Christian doctrine. He was to "command [*paraggellō*, a military term for issuing orders] certain men not to teach false doctrine." There was to be no reticence on his part

---

1. Myth is contrary to truth. "There is no denying the force of the assertion that if myth means non-historical make-believe or fairy tales or the product of the human inventiveness, there is no evidence that the writers interpreted the gospel in this way. Quite the opposite, as the Pastoral Epistles (1 Tim. 1:4, 4:7, 2 Tim. 4:4) make clear." I. Howard Marshall, ed., *New Testament Interpretation*, p. 240.

about the Christian truth and the way of the Christian life. The ill-conceived opinions of the heretical teachers needed to be exposed and counteracted.

The self-appointed teachers whom Timothy was to combat are described in three ways.

1. These teachers missed the mark of truth (1:6). Being pre-occupied with "myths and endless genealogies," they swerved from (*astocheō*) the practical and moral concerns of the Christian way of life. What these people taught was false, but their teaching also diverted attention from the importance of disciplined Christian living to useless talk. They had missed the path of truth and evidently thrived on novelties. So like the Athenians of old they "spent their time doing nothing but talking about and listening to the latest ideas" (Acts 17:21). The new has its place, but it should never be used to make God's eternal truths nebulous.

2. The false teachers were given to speculations that go astray (1:6). The heretical teachers had turned away (*ektrepō*) to meaningless talk. They refused to "put up with sound doctrine" (2 Tim. 4:3). Their minds were not open to the truth revealed through the apostles and prophets. As is characteristic of human nature, they preferred vigorous debates to sacrificial living. They were sidetracked from the discipline of Christian living and devoted themselves to meaningless speculations and empty talk.

3. The false teachers desired to teach the law (1:7). These self-styled experts in the Mosaic law were unqualified to teach it in the church. If taken seriously, their interpretations would have made the Christians slaves to the law. Their failure was to understand the law from the Christian point of view. Their ambition was to set themselves up as authoritative teachers, but their teachings were misguided. They did not understand what they talked about or the significance of the things they confidently affirmed.

This is not uncommon today. In most fields of knowledge we demand that a person have a certain understanding before he is permitted to lay down the law. But there are those who dogmatize biblical teaching without careful study of the Scriptures and without coming to an understanding of the backgrounds and languages of God's Word. Ignorant dogmatism continues to be a curse to the church.

D. Promote God's Work (1:5)

The heretical teachers promoted controversies rather than God's work. Their speculative teachings failed to edify the Ephesian church.

1. The purpose of the charge. The charge given by Paul to Timothy was to not antagonize the erring teachers. They were to be rebuked, but they were still people for whom God cared. Timothy's purpose was not to drive them out of the church but to call forth love. His exhortations were to establish and maintain a climate of love among the Christians. That stood as a contrast to the strife and divisions created by those given to empty talk. Disciplinary problems existed in the church, but the real purpose for dealing with those who had erred was to win them back to the truth. The whole design of the charge was love, the source of which Paul makes clear.

2. Love issues from (ek, "out of") two sources.
a. A pure heart (kardia). In Scripture the term *heart* refers to man's total affections. Of course the heart can be impure and in that condition it will produce hatred and malice, but the Holy Spirit can wash it clean with love (Rom. 1:24; 5:5). From a clean heart springs love. By the renewing of the Holy Spirit new power and affection are planted in the heart. There comes from a pure heart love that shows itself in kindness and that is devoted to the truth.
b. A good conscience (suneidēsis). The word *conscience* literally means "a knowing with" and refers to knowledge shared with one's self. It is the power to judge as to whether conduct is right or wrong. To the Sanhedrin Paul could say, "My brothers, I have fulfilled my duty to God in all good conscience to this day" (Acts 23:1). He broadens his claim by saying to Felix, "So I strive always to keep my conscience clear before God and man" (Acts

24:16; cf. 2 Tim. 1:3).[2] The conscience, however, is not an infallible guide. When men depart from the truth, their consciences can be seared or hardened so that they are not safe guides (1 Tim. 4:2).

To have a good conscience is to be able to look at our thoughts and actions without shame or guilt. Basic to a good conscience is the unmerited favor of God that blots out guilt and an openness to the guidance of the Holy Spirit. The Spirit directs us to keep God's law in deed and thought. The summation of the law is love. Love springs from a good conscience—a conscience that does not contemplate thoughts and actions contrary to God's law. Love is the fulfilling of the law.

c. A sincere faith (pistis). This is faith free of hypocrisy and play-acting. There is no need or room for pretense in genuine faith. Sincere faith is rooted and grounded in the Word of God, and love is the fruit of it. This simply means that with sincerity the truth is accepted and that such faith motivates us to communicate the gospel, which inevitably produces love in those who accept its truths.

No doubt the false teachers had neglected a pure heart, a good conscience, and a sincere faith. Like many people today, they had not been gripped by the essentials of the faith and had entangled themselves in endless argument and doctrinal errors to the detriment of the gospel. They failed to promote God's work.

III. The Law and Its Real Purpose (1:8-11)

A vital concern of the early Christians was the proper function of the law in the Christian faith. The false teachers, with their legalistic interpretations and speculations, had abused the law of Moses.[3] They made it a yoke of bondage and detrimental

---

2. No distinction should be made between "a good conscience" and "a clear conscience."

3. Some scholars take the word *law* here to refer to the Mosaic law; others to the law in general. Since the article is present with the word *law* in verse 8, and the lawbreakers of verses 9 and 10 follow the Ten Commandments rather closely, the reference is likely to the Mosaic law.

rather than helpful. That was, in fact, contrary to God's intent in giving the law. Elsewhere Paul declares that the law had a good purpose—to prepare people for Christ (Gal. 3:24). Observe what Paul says about the essential nature of the law and for whom it is designed.

A. The Law Is Good in Itself (1:8)

Paul argues that the law is essentially good, but is even more than that. The Greek (*kalos*, "admirable") calls attention also to the beauty of the law. Paul had no desire to deny the admirable precepts of the Mosaic law and its high standard. It was a law that God had given. Surely it had retarded many evils. Christ came not to destroy the law but to fulfill it (Matt. 5:17).

The law is an excellent thing "if a man uses it properly" (*nomimōs*, "lawfully"). The law, as good as it was, had been misused and misapplied by the "teachers of the law" (v. 7). There is a lawful use of it—the restraint of evil and the exposure of man's spiritual and moral bankruptcy without Christ. It is not, as the teachers of the law apparently tried to make it, a substitute for the gospel or the means by which sinners can be saved. It displays God's standard and thus reveals man's need.

B. The Law Is for Bad People (1:9-10a)

The design of the law is for the grossly wicked rather than for a good person (*dikaios*, "a righteous person"). A righteous person is in Jesus Christ and a true Christian. The Mosaic law is used improperly if it is imposed on Christians. This does not mean that it has no value at all for them, but the law "can no longer apply as a positive standard of conduct."[4] Indeed the legal restraints of the law are powerless to make Christians holier. It is the grace of God in the gospel, applied by the Holy Spirit, that motivates Christians to walk in holiness. The guide of Christians is the Holy Spirit, who is greater than the law.

The law is God's standard of righteousness, but its design is

---

4. Donald Guthrie, *The Pastoral Epistles*, (Tyndale New Testament Commentaries), p. 61.

for sinful men. And here Paul set out a list of the grossly wicked people.

1. *"Lawbreakers"* (anomoi, *"lawless"*) and *"rebels"* (anupotaktoi, *"disobedient"*). Ordinarily, lawless persons are not those who know nothing about the law but those who live as though there were no law. They are a law to themselves, living as they please and acting as though there were no divine law. Of course, those who do not hesitate to violate the moral law are also disobedient and rebellious. They recognize and submit to no authority above themselves. Discipline and control are given no place in their experience. They love to satisfy their own ambitions and desires, refusing to accept or obey any authority.

2. *The "ungodly"* (asebeis) *and "sinful"* (hamartōloi). To be godly is to live with a sense of reverence for God and His law. Godless people withhold from God reverence that is rightfully His. All men and women exist to glorify God and to enjoy Him forever, but the ungodly fall far short of this goal. Before Paul experienced saving grace he had been numbered among the ungodly, that is, among those who opposed God and who need a Savior. His conversion is the proof that "Christ Jesus came into the world to save sinners." He goes on to say, "of whom I am chief" (1:15, KJV).

3. *The "unholy"* (anosioi) *and "irreligious"* (bebēloi). These people deny sacred things. Such persons violate the ultimate sanctities and decencies of life. Sacred things are not important to the unholy. They do not hesitate to walk on that which is holy and sacred. Trampling under their feet the sacred, they desecrate the Lord's Day, belittle worship, and show no respect for God.

4. *Murderers of fathers* (patrolōiai) *and mothers* (mētrolōiai). A son or daughter who loses gratitude or respect for his or her parents violates the commandment: "Honor your father and your mother" (Exod. 20:12). Exodus 21:15 (KJV) says, "And he that smiteth his father, or his mother, shall be surely put to death." Striking a parent was punishable by death. How much more serious is patricide or matricide? It is the most outrageous violation of the fifth commandment.

5. *"Murderers"* (androphonoi, *"manslayers"*). In view here is the sixth commandment: "Thou shalt not kill" (Exod. 20:13, KJV). This commandment does not refer to manslaughter but rather to homicide. Since man is created in the image and likeness of God, his life is sacred. Unlawful taking of his life is an assault on the divine image in which he is created. It is well to remember that Christ gave the commandment—"Thou shalt not kill"—a broader meaning. Strong anger at a brother stands in violation of the spirit of this commandment (Matt. 5:21–22).

6. *Immoral persons* (pornoi, *"adulterers"*; arsenokoitai, *"perverts"*). The seventh commandment states, "Thou shalt not commit adultery" (Exod. 20:14, KJV). Unnatural vices and low standards of sexual morality were widespread in the ancient world. Into that world Christianity brought a new virtue— chastity. Adultery was bad enough, but Paul speaks of one of the worst forms of immorality when he uses the word "perverts" (*arsenokoitai*). This word is composed of two words: "male" (*arsēn*) and "bed" (*koitē*). The reference must be to male homosexuals, that is, sodomites, as referred to in Romans 1:27, "... the men also abandoned natural relations with women and were inflamed with lust for one another."

7. *Menstealers* (andrapodistai). This is a violation of the eighth commandment: "Thou shalt not steal." In the first-century world the kidnaping of slaves was a profitable crime. That was one of the worst forms of stealing. A kidnaper is a thief who makes merchandise of human life (Deut. 24:7). What he steals is the most precious of all things on the earth.[5]

8. *"Liars"* (pseustai) *and "perjurers"* (epiorkoi). "Thou shalt not bear false witness against thy neighbor" is the ninth commandment. Transgressors of this commandment are liars and out of harmony with the truth. By disposition man is inclined to practice deception (Rom. 3:13). His lying and twisting of the truth are evident in both word and deed. Often his actions fail to coincide with his confession.

---

5. Martin Dibelius and Hans Conzelmann, *The Pastoral Epistles*, p. 23.

A form of lying is perjury. This is done under oath, when a falsehood is asserted to be true. The word of a liar or a perjurer cannot be trusted. Lying is not simply an act; it is a condition and manifests itself in individual lies. This condition robs man of his own genuineness. He has only a counterfeit existence. "Only where the lie is exposed by the truth of Christ and man comes under the Lordship of Christ and becomes a new man can counterfeit existence based on deceit and untruth be overcome."[6]

C. The Law Is for Those Who Oppose the
   Sound Doctrine (1:10b–11)

The various classes of sinners for whom the law has been designed have been identified. Paul goes on to indicate the relevance of the law to any other sin: "and for whatever else is contrary to the sound doctrine." The law is for criminals, but here the apostle speaks of teaching intended for the normal rule of life. That rule is none other than "the sound doctrine" that conforms to the gospel of glory.

1. The sound doctrine. The word (*hugiainousa*) translated as "sound" means "wholesome" or "healthful." As the Pastoral Epistles make clear, wholesome teaching plays a vital part in the health and the purity of the church. At Crete Titus was admonished to hold firmly to the trustworthy message, so that he could encourage others by sound doctrine and refute those who oppose it (Titus 1:9; cf. 2:1; 2 Tim. 4:3). Sound instruction agrees with godliness (1 Tim. 6:3). All Scripture, we are told, is inspired by God and is useful for teaching, rebuking, correcting, and training in righteousness (2 Tim. 3:16). Sound doctrine is healthful because it promotes spiritual growth and health. Every sin is a sin against sound doctrine, but wholesome Christian living is rooted in wholesome teaching.

2. The gospel of glory. Sound doctrine is in conformity with the gospel. "'The gospel' is thus a summary of Christian doctrine,

---

6. Colin Brown, ed., *The New International Dictionary of New Testament Theology,* vol. 2, p. 474.

proclamation, and teaching."[7] It tells of the glory of the blessed God. The phrase *gospel of glory,* which reflects the literal Greek, is sometimes rendered "glorious gospel."[8] That translation is misleading and transfers the glory from God, the central figure of redemption, so that the stress falls on the nature of the redemptive message. Here the emphasis is placed on the mighty works of God in the person of Christ. The gospel is the glory of God and its manifestation is in the face of Jesus Christ (2 Cor. 4:4-6).[9] God acted mightily in Christ, and God's own glory was revealed in His Son's life, death, and resurrection. What the gospel proclaims is the mighty redemptive work of Christ in which is seen the perfections of God. The gospel is concerned with the mighty saving acts of God and is, therefore, "the gospel of the glory of the blessed God."

Sound doctrine according to the gospel has been committed to all Christians' trust as it had been to Paul. The importance of sound Christian doctrine cannot be stressed too much; it issues forth in spiritual vigor and growth. As already noted, the law itself has its proper place in the church, but there were those in the Ephesian church who used the law in the wrong way, seeking to make it an absolute guide for Christians. The law set forth the standard of right and speaks loudly to the sinner. "Law is a sort of medicine, only to be applied where the moral nature is diseased; Christian teaching is a healthy food for healthy people, a means of joy, freedom, larger activity."[10]

IV. Conclusion

A crisis of truth existed in the church at Ephesus. False teachers had arisen among the Christians and with their fanciful

---

7. C. K. Barrett, *The Pastoral Epistles,* (The New English Bible), p. 44.

8. See the King James Version, Revised Standard Version, Phillips, and the New International Version.

9. There is no need of taking the genitive (*doxēs*) in 1 Timothy 1:11 as descriptive: "glorious gospel." It is a genitive of content and the phrase *to euaggelion tēs doxēs tou makariou theou* is to be translated as "the gospel, the content of which is the glory of the blessed God."

10. E. F. Scott, *The Pastoral Epistles,* (The Moffatt New Testament Commentary), pp. 10-11.

interpretations they were undermining sound doctrine. They had been overcome by the temptation of novelty and had set their heads to inventing up-to-date doctrine. They were the fashion designers in theology, and they modeled, along with their "sick" doctrine on the law, some of the most outrageous fashions—"myths and endless genealogies."

Doctrinal novelties and new teachings have their attraction, even in the church. As Paul advised young Timothy, we must follow the pattern of sound teaching and guard the truth that has been entrusted to us by the Holy Spirit (2 Tim. 1:13–14). Jesus once warned against those who pass human traditions off as the truth—"their teachings are but rules taught by men" (Matt. 15:9). Every Christian must take care not to distort God's Word by his own opinions or by the views of others. It is possible to be taken "captive through hollow and deceptive philosophy, which depends on human tradition and basic principles of this world rather than on Christ" (Col. 2:8). Those who are entrapped twist the Scriptures to their own destruction (2 Peter 3:16).

There is a need for defending Christian truth, but the majority of Christians cannot congratulate themselves on their ability to distinguish between doctrinal soundness and phoniness. Confusion prevails about basic Christian truth and secular ways of thinking contrary to the Christian faith. Much of this may be traced to the influence of the thinking of preachers and theologians, who have subordinated the Word of God to the current thinking of sociologists, psychologists, and philosophers. From pulpits we hear often nothing but a sugar-coated philosophy or ideas that impress us with the ingenuity of the preacher. Christians need to draw on contemporary insights, but these applications must be made in a way that is consistent with the supreme authority of Scripture.

A vital connection exists between sound doctrine and the church's mission of ministering to the needs of people. Understanding the human condition from the biblical perspective will help us avoid blundering in our Christian service. The teachings of Christ and His unique and absolute claims as Savior cannot be disconnected from a vibrant living faith. The early disciples "continued stedfastly in the apostles' doctrine" (Acts 2:42, KJV).

The Christian has been entrusted with God's message, which

by its very power can bring life and death, salvation and judgment to those who hear. No one was more acutely aware of this than Paul. That is why he urged Titus to "hold firmly to the trustworthy message as it has been taught, so that he can encourage others by sound doctrine and refute those who oppose it" (Titus 1:9). The truth of the gospel was and still is clearly the doctrinal standard to be preserved jealously.

3

Our Vocation

(1:12–20)

The gospel was a powerful reality in Paul's own experience and life. This led him to speak about his vocation as a preacher and servant of Jesus Christ. God's mercy had been shown to him. He had endured suffering as a "soldier" of the Lord (2 Tim. 2:3–10). He had kept the faith and lived a life worthy of imitation (2 Tim. 3:10–15).

Never could the apostle forget the magnitude of God's grace that cleansed him from his old sins and healed him of spiritual blindness. With that in mind, he wrote that God "has saved us and called us to a holy life—not because of anything we have done but because of his own purpose and grace" (2 Tim. 1:9). He had been called both to be saved and to serve, which, in fact, is fundamental to the vocation of a Christian. However, the child of God is not merely to bear witness to the gospel but also to be a living evidence of its meaning and power.

Consider what a difference Christ made when He changed Paul's character and appointed him a servant of the gospel.

I. Gratitude for Paul's Calling (1:12-14)

On the road to Damascus Paul experienced God's transforming grace. It does not seem that Paul ever ceased to marvel at this experience in which he saw ". . . the light of the knowledge of the glory of God in the face of Christ" (2 Cor. 4:6). He had deserved nothing, but he received an abundance of grace. Just for him to recall the sins of his past kept the flame of gratitude burning in his heart.

A. Paul's Former State (1:13)

Spontaneously Paul broke out in thanksgiving and praise for the blessings that he had received. The ground for his gratitude was manifold, but the emphasis falls upon the saving grace of Christ. Paul had displayed three characteristics.

1. A blasphemer. Before his conversion Paul threw his angry words and ridicule at the Christians and accused them of crimes against God. Heaping on innocent Christians his insults and outrage, he tried to force them to blaspheme (Acts 26:11). But he was the blasphemer, and they were the victims of his malicious insults.

2. A persecutor. As an instigator and conductor of persecution against the Christians, Paul went even to foreign cities to persecute them (Acts 26:11). Acts 9:1 pictures his violent aggression against them: "Meanwhile, Saul was still breathing out murderous threats against the Lord's disciples." The risen Lord was so personally identified with His persecuted people that He asked Paul, "Saul, Saul, why do you persecute me?" (Acts 9:4). By physical violence Paul had sought to exterminate the church from the face of the earth (Gal. 1:13). He never forgot that he had vented his rage upon Christ and the church.

3. "A violent man." The word (*hubristēs*) refers to a spiteful, insolent man who is inflated with pride and engages in the most outrageous insults and acts. Stronger than the word *blasphemer,* this term expresses Paul's deep contempt for the Christians and his atrocious acts against them. Modern psychologists would call this sadism, a delight in inflicting pain upon others.

B. Special Mercy Toward Paul (1:13–14)

Such an objectionable person as Paul obtained the mercy of God. Wrought in the heart of that deeply guilty man was God's miracle of grace.

1. Paul had acted in "ignorance and unbelief" (1:13b). In his outrage against the church Paul thought that he was doing God a service, not knowing that the church had been purchased by the life of God's Son. The Nazarene sect, so he thought, should be destroyed (Acts 26:9). His acts of aggression were motivated by the ignorance of unbelief, but even the wrongs done in ignorance were covered by God's sovereign provision of mercy. However, there are limits to God's patience with ignorance. "In the past God overlooked such ignorance, but now he commands all people everywhere to repent" (Acts 17:30).

2. Paul received an overflow of God's grace (1:14). Grace was central in Paul's thought and life. Interestingly, he uses a compound word (*huperepleonasen*) to express the surplus of grace over sin. This superabundance of grace recalls the words of Romans 5:20, "where sin increased, grace increased all the more." Since a good man does not deserve grace, certainly a blasphemer, a persecutor, a violent man does not. Yet the saving grace of God touched Paul and transformed the very heart of his life—his motives, desires, and ambitions. A radical change was wrought in him, and he became a new creation.

The evidence of God's grace in Paul's experience was "faith and love." Divine grace works through faith and love, both of which are found in a living relationship with Jesus Christ. A life that is inspired by the kind of faith and love found in Jesus Christ is possible only through God's grace.

The sins of Paul were black, but in the midst of his rebellion against God there was an overflowing measure of grace. A real temptation for Christ's followers is to limit the power of divine grace. It is so easy for us to expect the conversion of only those who have the right background or training. The miracle of superabounding grace that Paul experienced has been repeated many times, even in our own day. On the basis of justice that miracle would not have occurred. Justice deals with people according to what they deserve, but grace goes beyond that and is not limited by calculated merits as justice is.

C. Paul's Heartfelt Thanksgiving (1:12)

To fulfill our vocation as Christians requires that we be fully endowed with divine power. There is no better model of this than Paul. His gratitude for divine grace is expressed in the thanksgiving for three tremendous blessings.

1. For strengthening him. Paul had learned that Christ never gives a person a task without giving him power to do it. The great apostle had been given strength for his ministry. He could never boast of what he had done but only of what Christ had enabled him to do. He had received power far beyond his own abilities. Everyone who is given a task by Christ receives strength to perform it.

2. For trusting him. Before conversion Paul had strongly opposed the church. The amazing fact was that the Lord chose Paul to be a Christian missionary and an apostle to the Gentiles. Not only did Christ forgive him, but He also entrusted Paul with the gospel. The past sins of that man did not make it impossible for Christ to trust him. When we tend to distrust people because of their past sins and failures, we need to recall that the arch-persecutor of the church, the chief of sinners, was made the ambassador of Christ and entrusted with the riches of the gospel.

3. For appointing him. The initiative came from God, who appointed Paul to the service (*diakonia,* "ministry") of the gospel. His ministry consisted of serving rather than being served. He was thankful for this appointment, though it involved hardships and dangers. The apostle recognized that the divine appointment was not to fame and honor but to service and sacrifice. His glory was in serving the gospel and the church. Everyone who has been reached by superabounding grace has been saved to serve.

II. God's Plan for the Salvation of Humanity (1:15-17)

All men and women can read Paul's account of his spiritual experience and be encouraged that they are not beyond the reach of God's saving grace. His conversion and his receiving of mercy should inspire confidence that the saving power of Christ is sufficient to blot out the blackest of sins. The experience of the chief of sinners affirms that there is hope for all.

A. The Reliability of Saving Truth (1:15a)

Before appealing to a familiar saying—"Christ Jesus came into the world to save sinners"—Paul called attention to its fundamental character.

1. A trustworthy saying. This expression occurs a number of times in the Pastoral Epistles (1 Tim. 3:1; 4:9; 2 Tim. 2:11; Titus 3:8) and can be rendered as "sure is the Word" (*pistos ho logos*). The idea is that the truth is absolutely reliable, wholly trustworthy. No doubt the truth that Paul was about to introduce was cited commonly in the churches.

2. Worthy of full acceptance. These words reinforce the central importance of the trustworthy saying—"Christ Jesus came into the world to save sinners." This saying was and still is worthy of universal acceptance. The absolute relevance of this truth makes it worthy to be wholeheartedly received by all. The application is broad, but rightly so. All are sinners, and Christ died for sinners.

B. The Essence of Truth: "Christ Jesus Came into the World to Save Sinners" (1:15b)

These words affirm the saving power of Jesus Christ and single out two important truths.

1. Christ's incarnation. What Christ did was entirely dependent on God's gracious initiative. God "... saved us and called us to a holy life—not because of anything we have done but because of his own purpose and grace" (2 Tim. 1:9). God sent His Son as Savior. The phrase "came into the world" emphasizes divine condescension. The Savior came from the heights of glory to the depths of humanity. He "made himself nothing, taking the very nature of a servant, being made in human likeness. And being found in appearance as a man, he humbled himself and became obedient to death—even death on a cross!" (Phil. 2:7–8). He descended, giving up His exalted state and taking on a lowly state far beneath His dignity and majesty.

2. Christ's mission. The purpose of divine condescension was to save sinners. The Savior came into the world. The term *world* here refers to the realm of evil, rather than to the physical universe. He came into the sphere where evil exercised tremendous influence and where fallen men lived, not, however, to save the "righteous," but sinners—people who are guilty of behaving contrary to God's will and living misdirected lives. The mission of Christ was summed up well when Paul said, "While we were still sinners, Christ died for us" (Rom. 5:8). The truth is that Christ saves sinners. His death does not help sinners to save themselves, nor does it persuade sinners to save themselves; rather, His death saves them. Indeed He came to seek and to save the lost.

C. The Magnitude of Saving Truth (1:15c–16)

Before Paul's conversion we would not have expected him to become a servant of Christ. The Savior transformed his life and showed what He could make out of unpromising material.

1. The worst of sinners. Conscious of the magnitude of God's grace, the apostle described himself as the foremost (*prōtos,* "first") of sinners. Never did he forget his previous sinful state. Every time he thought of the greatness of his sins, he also was reminded of the greatness of the saving grace of Christ.

Before his conversion Paul had lived according to the rigid standards of the Pharisees (Acts 26:5; cf. Phil. 3:5). He had been dedicated to the strictest sect in Judaism. How could he describe himself as "the worst of sinners"? Were there not greater sinners than Paul? He surveyed his life before conversion, and realized how atrocious and brutal his sins had been against the church and the Lord. In light of God's holiness and his past he was a sinner of the highest order. He had been zealous for the law, but his reaction to Christianity was fanatical in that he became a blasphemer, a persecutor, and a violent man. His terrible crimes against the people of God were sufficient reason for ranking himself as foremost of sinners. He was a great sinner but Christ is a great Savior.

2. An example of Christ's saving power and patience. The chief of sinners received mercy. He had vented his hostility on the church. His conversion was proof of Christ's unlimited long-suffering.[1] Christ dealt with the great persecutor in patience and withheld divine wrath and judgment. He permitted His adversary to continue to breathe out slaughter against the people of God until He brought him to faith. In His long-suffering, Christ offered an example (*hupotupōsis,* "sketch, model") that should prevent any unsaved person from despairing of receiving divine mercy.

No conversion has been as effective as Paul's in pointing souls to the Savior. There is hope for all sinners, even for those counted among the most wretched and guilty of the most shameful deeds. The foremost of sinners received mercy. He is the model, reminding us of Christ's unlimited patience and saving power.

D. The Supremacy of God (1:17)

As Paul thought about what God had done—bestowing on him eternal life and calling him to a vocation that rests in the divine initiative of love and reconciliation—his heart overflowed in adoration. Just a reflection on God's mercies and power called forth an outburst of praise.

1. God is "the King eternal." This phrase also can be translated as "King of the ages" or "King of eternity." The Jews divided time into two ages—the present age and the age to come. God is King of both spheres. Through all ages God remains sovereign and is "the blessed and only Ruler, the King of kings and Lord of lords" (1 Tim. 6:15). A prime example of this is God's overrule of Paul's design to destroy the church. The Lord of the ages will suffer man to persist in his rebellion against the divine will, but ultimately God's purpose will prevail. One thing is certain: every person is on his way to judgment in which he must face the sovereign Lord.

---

1. The word (*hapas,* "all") translated as "unlimited" in the New International Version stands in the attributive position and signifies "the total sum of Christ's long-suffering" or "the perfect patience of which he is capable." See Robert Hanna, *A Grammatical Aid to the Greek New Testament,* vol. 2, p. 134.

2. God is immortal and invisible. By nature He is immortal. He is outside of the physical sphere, not subject to the process of change. All creatures of time are corruptible. Decay and death are part of their experience. God is imperishable, being the same yesterday, today, and forever. At His first coming Christ "... destroyed death and ... brought life and immortality to light through the gospel" (2 Tim. 1:10). Beyond death God grants the gift of immortality to His people (1 Cor. 15:53–55). All that is visible is perishable; but God is invisible. God can only be seen by the eyes of faith.

3. God—eternal, immortal, and invisible—is the only God. This truth is clearly expressed in the ancient Shema—"Hear, O Israel: The LORD our God, the LORD is one" (Deut. 6:4). Numerically God is one and is incomprehensible in His matchless unity. The only God is due our worship into the ages of ages and is to be praised with our lips and in our lives forever.

III. Commitment of a Charge to Timothy (1:18–20)

God's grace had saved and called Paul to the work of ministry. That should have inspired Timothy, who also had been set apart for an important work. To encourage his young friend to be faithful to the message and ministry committed to him, Paul reminded him to view the charge from two perspectives (1:3–11).

A. A Look Backward (1:18a)

Paul was a man who had been marked out by the prophets. It was through the prophets that the message came, "Set apart for me Barnabas and Saul for the work to which I have called them" (Acts 13:2). Likewise Timothy had been marked out by Christian prophets as a man who had a call on his life.[2] Perhaps

---

2. Some commentators understand the words "prophecies once made about you" to be a reference to Timothy's ordination and call attention to the admonition of 1 Timothy 4:14, "Do not neglect your gift, which was given you through a prophetic message when the body of elders laid their hands on you." See George A.

the prophecies were made either at Lystra where he entered the church or at the time he became an associate of Paul. The prophetic utterances concerned Timothy's call to the ministry, with divine promises of strength for the work of the kingdom.

The "instruction" (*paraggelia,* "charge") that urged Timothy to be diligent in ministry was not new. It was a reaffirmation of the prophecies that had singled him out as an ambassador of the gospel. Timothy was not beyond need of Paul's charge and reminder of the divine initiative in calling him to ministry. Any Christian—no matter how devoted to Christ—can become discouraged, weary, and fainthearted. A stirring exhortation to look back and recall what God has done can fill a real need.

B. A Look Forward (1:18b–20)

The prophetic utterances assured Timothy of divine help to carry on his work. God had chosen Timothy as Paul's successor. Aware of that, the apostle called on the young man to be a faithful soldier of Jesus Christ. The fulfillment of his mission required that he wage a good fight—a fight free of carnal methods and unworthy ends, and against evil and doctrinal perversions. He was to use two weapons in such noble warfare.

1. Armed with faith. Without faith in God it is impossible to be a Christian, but the word *faith* here seems to refer to right belief. By holding the faith delivered to the saints, Timothy would not compromise the truth but would fight gallantly to maintain its integrity. Every Christian soldier needs faith, right belief, so that he can withstand perversions of the gospel.

2. Armed with a good conscience. Truth and the moral life go hand in hand. A good conscience is free from charges of hypocrisy and springs from living in accordance with what we profess. The conscience can be disobeyed, ignored, or even seared with a hot iron (1 Tim. 4:2). A person who has a good conscience has been renewed by the Holy Spirit and his practice affirms holy doctrine. Teaching the Word of God is good, but the truth must

---

Buttrick, ed., *The Interpreter's Bible,* vol. 11, p. 394, and Anthony T. Hanson, *The Pastoral Letters,* (The Cambridge Bible Commentary), pp. 29–30.

shape and fashion our lives so that it is not compromised by our conduct. In short, that is characteristic of a good conscience.

3. *The peril of rejecting the faith and a good conscience.* "'More often than we know, religious error has its roots in moral rather than in intellectual causes.' The converse is equally true, for faulty belief not infrequently leads to moral disaster."[3] What we believe and how we live are inseparably related—to reject faith (right belief) is to reject a good conscience. To reject a good conscience indicates that faith is shipwrecked. Faith not only must be professed but also must be lived.

a. *Hymenaeus and Alexander.*[4] These men were examples of those who had made shipwreck of their faith. They turned away from the truth and lost their right to a good conscience. They abandoned their ministerial charge.[5] In short, the result was spiritual and moral bankruptcy. Having abandoned their vocation and faith, they became ministerial tragedies. The same happens today when Christians reject the leading of their consciences and accordingly "have shipwrecked their faith."

b. *Disciplinary action.* The will of God was for the salvation of Hymenaeus and Alexander. God "wants all men to be saved and to come to a knowledge of the truth." Christ "gave himself as a ransom for all men" (1 Tim. 2:4, 6). The words of Paul indicate that in dealing with these men strong disciplinary action was taken—"whom I have handed over to Satan to be taught not to blaspheme." This reminds us of Paul's instruction to the Corinthian believers to hand over to Satan a man guilty of having an affair with his stepmother "so that the sinful nature may be destroyed and his spirit saved on the day of the Lord" (1 Cor. 5:5). Apparently deliverance to Satan involved exclusion from the fellowship of believers. Expulsion from the church thrust Hymenaeus and Alexander out into the world, the domain of

---

3. Donald Guthrie, *The Pastoral Epistles,* (Tyndale New Testament Commentaries), p. 68.

4. Hymenaeus is mentioned also in 2 Timothy 2:17. The Alexander in 2 Timothy 4:14 was a metalworker and probably is not the same as in 1 Timothy. Alexander was a common name in the first century.

5. The context implies that both Hymenaeus and Alexander had received the same ministerial charge that had been given to Timothy.

Satan. Cut off from the fellowship of believers, they were no longer protected by the body of Christ from satanic attacks. They experienced the buffeting and the afflictions of Satan.

Yet such discipline was necessary that they might "be taught not to blaspheme." Barring Hymenaeus and Alexander from the church was in the interest of correction and reclamation. The action was disciplinary, but it was not motivated by vengeance. The apostle's design was not to put them out of the church and let them go to hell but to re-establish them in the faith. Having handed those men over to Satan, Paul hoped that they would be brought to their senses and would abandon their heresy and live in accordance with the truth. The purpose was to reclaim and save them, not destroy them.

Seldom is church discipline invoked in our day. The neglect of disciplinary action where there is departure from the cardinal biblical truths or where there is guilt for deeds of immorality has devastating effects on the spiritual health of the church and on individual Christians. Discipline for doctrinal error and outrageous sins has its place in the church, but it should be administered in a way that encourages those who have made shipwreck to find their way back to the Savior and the church.

IV. Conclusion

Vocation is from God. That was Paul's experience. God summoned him into His service. Paul was a blasphemer, a persecutor, and a violent man, but God did not consider him too bad to become a Christian and to do the work of an apostle. God's grace made him altogether a new man and commissioned him to declare the gospel.

Paul was called both to have a "share in the heavenly inheritance" and to serve in this world. As a Christian he was to do his duty here as a citizen of the coming Kingdom of God. The longer Paul lived and served the gospel, the more grateful he was for the power of Christ and His truth. Indeed he was thankful for his calling—God had deemed him trustworthy to be appointed to the work of the ministry and had strengthened him for the task.

All Christians have a vocation. They are called into a living relationship with God and with the community of believers. They are to believe in the mighty acts of God in Christ and to live in responsible obedience to God wherever they are. The apostle Paul was deeply aware that the divine call to service, common to all Christians, is rooted in this truth: "Christ Jesus came into the world to save sinners." What God did in His Son restores us to fellowship with Himself. As we live and serve in this world we are to see, as Paul did, every person as "one for whom Christ died." The cross of Christ is precisely the way God deals with the realities of sin and death. Those who have come to faith in Christ are justified and sanctified and are brought into His service.

Our call is to holiness. God calls us out of the world to share in the heavenly inheritance—eternal life itself. At the same time the call is to service in the world. Here in this life other voices call. Hymenaeus and Alexander heard these other voices in their day. They failed to distinguish God's call from the other voices and ceased "holding on to faith and a good conscience." They made shipwreck, compromising sincere conviction and disobeying the voice of a good conscience. When we become unsure of our calling and compromise our commitment to the Christian life, defeat follows. But we are called to fight a good fight and to maintain and to transmit the faith. That is precisely our vocation. Be faithful to it and maintain it at all cost. The fulfillment of our calling redounds to the praise and glory of "the King eternal, immortal, invisible, the only God."

4

Public Worship and Order

(2)

The Christian church is a worshiping fellowship. From the very beginning that has been a mark of the church. Scriptures clearly testify to this. It was the practice of both Christ and the apostles to worship and preach in the synagogues wherever they went. The early believers devoted themselves to the breaking of bread together (a reference to the celebration of the Lord's Supper) and to common prayer (Acts 2:42). The church has rendered many services to mankind, but above all it has united Christian men and women in the worship of almighty God, Creator, Redeemer, and Judge.

Public worship is both a privilege and a responsibility. Indeed it is a great privilege to worship the Lord in the congregation of believers and to magnify Him for His manifold benefits. At church lives can be refreshed and peace can be found through the worship of God and fellowship with His people.

At the same time the participation in public worship is also a most solemn responsibility. The proper end of all worship is the glory of God. Keenly aware that worship was a serious matter, Paul gave Timothy instructions, stressing the centrality of prayer in worship and insisting that all things in worship must be done in a decent and orderly fashion.

I. Centrality of Prayer (2:1-2a)

The words "first of all," along with "I urge," stress the central importance of communion with God. For Paul prayer was a vital element of worship, and he laid word upon word here when he spoke of public prayer and Christian worship.

A. A Variety of Terms (2:1b)

The words used to identify the elements of prayer—supplications, prayers, intercessions, and thanksgiving—are more or less synonyms, but they add emphasis to the importance of this spiritual exercise. Distinctions between the terms should not be pressed too much, but some differences can be discerned.

1. Supplications (deēsis). These are requests or entreaties for specific needs. An awareness of a human need awakens within us the desire to make a request. The petitioner knows that only God can supply that need. So he prays, with a real sense of personal insufficiency, that the need will be met. True supplication always begins with the realization of our helplessness. God is humbly entreated to give His blessings. The need may be for the healing of a person's spirit or body, or for good relationships within the church and the home, or for reconciliation of nations on the verge of war.

2. Prayer (proseuchē). This is a more general word for prayer.[1] Since it is in the list, its meaning may be restrictive. Supplication (*deēsis*) may be addressed to either man or God. Prayer (*proseuchē*) is never offered to anyone but God. Man reaches out to God in prayer and approaches Him for help. He realizes that there are certain needs that only God can satisfy. Conscious that only God can effectually minister to his particular needs, the believer turns to Him in prayer. It is well to remember that there are needs that only God can touch. Only God can grant forgiveness of sins. Only God can give special strength to live the Christian life. Only God can enable us to

---

1. See Colin Brown, ed., *The New International Dictionary of New Testament Theology*, vol. 2, p. 861.

discern the riches of the gospel and to come to grips with His truth. Do we turn toward God believing that He will turn toward us?

3. *Intercession* (enteuxis). The word *intercession* includes ideas such as "meeting with," "coming together," "access," "audience," and "petition." The fundamental idea is prayer in behalf of others. Compassion frequently takes the form of intercessory prayer in the Christian community. Intercession may be promoted by the need and the suffering of the world. It may be an expression of heartfelt affection and concern for others in the Christian community. The apostle Paul wrote to Timothy, ". . . night and day I constantly remember you in my prayers" (2 Tim. 1:3). Our petitions should express a genuine concern for others.

4. *Thanksgiving* (eucharistia). The prayers of thanksgiving are expressions of gratitude, offered by the congregation in public worship, but Christians need not restrict thanksgiving to the worship at the house of God.[2] Thanksgiving is integral to prayer, but often it is a lost element in prayer. As Paul wrote to the Philippian Christians, ". . . in everything, by prayer and petition, with thanksgiving, present your requests to God" (Phil. 4:6). Prayer is not merely asking God for blessings but is "giving thanks to the Father, who has qualified you to share in the inheritance of the saints . . ." (Col. 1:12). All blessings from the hands of God are undeserved and are grounds for us to offer thanks. We have the right to bring our petitions, needs, and desires to God; but we also have a duty to express sincere gratitude to God for His sovereign deeds in creation, for His mighty saving acts in Jesus Christ, for the abundance of His gifts, and for His unfailing faithfulness.

B. Universal Scope (2:1c–2a)

The interest of Paul went far beyond the Christian community. His sweeping assertions leave no doubt about this: "God our

---

2. Donald A. Hagner and Murray J. Harris, eds., *Pauline Studies*, p. 60.

Savior . . . wants *all men* to be saved" (v. 3, italics added). Christ ". . . gave himself as a ransom for *all men"* (v. 6, italics added). "I want *men everywhere* to lift up holy hands in prayer" (v. 8, italics added). Prayer is to be offered "for *everyone*—for kings and *all those* in authority" (v. 2, italics added). The Christian is not to confine his prayers to narrow interests.

1. All men. Prayer is universal and should be all-inclusive. At Paul's time the church could have been tempted to turn in upon itself and become preoccupied with itself rather than its mission. The threat of the heretical teachers in the Ephesian church could have disposed that congregation to shield itself from paganism by withdrawing into itself.[3] Of course that would have been betrayal of the central truth of the gospel that Jesus Christ "gave himself a ransom for all men." To counter this temptation the church was to include all men in its prayers, touching the whole realm of human interests.

God's mercy is universal, and He desires that Christians pray for all men—believers and unbelievers, every ethnic and racial group, every man, woman, and child. The church is to pray for the whole human race.

2. Kings[4] and those in positions of authority. Barring the character and disposition of the officials of state, the church is to pray for them. There could be a tendency among Christians to leave them out of their devotions, especially when rulers are openly hostile.

It is possible that Nero was the emperor of the Roman Empire

---

3. The emphasis on universality could have been due to gnostic tendencies toward exclusiveness, placing undue stress on knowledge (1 Tim. 6:20) and distinguishing between the spiritual and the natural (Jude 19), but verses 5–7 suggest that it was due to Jewish exclusiveness. Naturally Paul was concerned that the Christian church not fail in fulfilling its mission to all men, as the Jews had done. Walter Lock, *The Pastoral Epistles,* (The International Critical Commentary), p. 24.

4. The plural "kings" is not likely a reference to a coruler, as has been suggested, and does not provide a true basis for dating the composition of 1 Timothy after A.D. 137. Here Paul is setting forth a general principle that rulers were to be included always in the prayers of the church without implying a time when co-emperors reigned in Rome.

when this letter was written. Even though he abused his authority and persecuted the church, the Christians were to pray for his well-being and for the country. When civil authority is abused by those in high positions, it is easy for Christians to have an unchristian attitude toward these people. The best prevention of this is to make them subjects of prayer.

The church's duty is to pray for those who are set in authority over the kingdoms of the earth and to bring all people before the throne of grace. "The basis of this is the 'one God . . . one mediator . . . a ransom for all.'"[5]

II. Purpose of Prayer (2:2b-7)

Prayer is the Christian's means of bringing about mighty results. An unbeliever may complain about circumstances or those placed over him, but the Christian can and must pray. By prayer he can influence the course of national affairs. Paul stated that there are two reasons for praying.

A. To Lead a Peaceful and Quiet Life (2:2b)

The focus is on the government and human relations. Freedom from the suspicion of civil authorities and from outward disturbances enables Christians to lead[6] peaceful and quiet lives.[7] This is a legitimate reason for Christians to pray for those in power. The gospel can be preached with more liberty where there is peace—freedom from war, freedom from persecution, freedom from rebellion.

An atmosphere of peace is conducive to godliness and holiness as well as to the proclamation of the gospel. Godliness (*eusebeia*) designates a vital spiritual relation with God and the kind of life that is pleasing to God. A godly person conducts

---

5. Alan G. Note, *Pastoral Letters,* (A New Testament Commentary), p. 509.

6. The verb that The New International Version translates as "may live" (*diagōmen*) is a compound and expresses here a perfective idea, "may live throughout our life."

7. The words "peaceful" (*ēremos*) and "quiet" (*hēsuchios*) are synonyms and stress the importance of tranquillity in social affairs.

himself in a way that shows a deep reverence for God. "Holiness" (*semnotēs*, "dignity") refers to the Christian's seriousness in outlook, which encompasses both doctrine and life. This quality of life gives dignity to a person and orderliness to his life. Such a person, William Barclay says, "moves through the world . . . as if the world was the temple of the living God. He never forgets the holiness of God or the dignity of man. He is the man whose attitude toward God and toward man is right."[8]

B. To Please God Our Savior (2:3)

Prayer for all, even rulers, is good and acceptable in the sight of God. This is in keeping with God's own saving character— "who wants all men to be saved and to come to a knowledge of the truth."[9] If that were not true, the prayers of God's people would have little value. But God does liberate from the power of guilt and sin, and He places on His people the responsibility to pray for the world at large. The universal scope of their intercessions has a fourfold basis.

1. There is one God (2:5a). This is a proclamation of the unity of God. The same fundamental truth is declared in Deuteronomy, which the Jews cited in every religious service—"Hear, O Israel, the LORD our God, the LORD is one." That is the basis of all intercessory prayer. Our petitions are to the one and only heavenly Father. Neither the Gnostics nor the pagans grasped this truth. The Gnostics insisted that there were two gods and that each was hostile to the other. The pagans believed that there were many gods. Both were in error. In reality there is only one God. There is not a god for the black man, a god for the white man, a god for the employer, a god for the employee, a god for the people, and a god for those in positions of authority.

---

8. *The Letters to Timothy, Titus and Philemon,* p. 71.

9. The compound word for "knowledge" (*epignōsis*) can appropriately be rendered as "full knowledge," involving both the intellect and heart, and is arrived at through faith and repentance. The phrase "knowledge of the truth," which is a technical term in the Pastorals (2 Tim. 2:25; 3:7; Titus 1:1), refers to the whole revelation of God in Christ. To know fully the ultimate reality disclosed in Jesus Christ is the aim of salvation.

If there were many gods, then each person would be left to pray to his own god. What we need to learn is that there is only one true God for mankind—for all nations, for all races, for all people. There is none like Him. He is the Creator of us all and desires that every person come to a knowledge of the truth. God's concern includes everyone, so prayer is to be offered to Him for everyone.

2. *There is one mediator (2:5b).* The mediator is the man Christ Jesus. For the Jews there were many mediators; they thought of angels as intermediaries. Modern men like to think that there are many ways to God, but there is only one mediator between God and man. "I am the way and the truth and the life," said Jesus. "No one comes to the Father except through me" (John 14:6).

Jesus Christ stood between God and man as a representative of both. Indeed He was qualified to be the Mediator, being God and man.[10] The eternal Son of God was manifested as a real man, and as the God-Man He performed the work of mediation, bringing God and man together in reconciliation. As a merciful and faithful high priest Christ atoned for the sins of mankind. That accomplishment for all affirms that there is only one mediator between God and man, the man Christ Jesus.

3. *One price is paid for the salvation of all (2:6).* The price the one mediator gave is stated in these words: "who gave himself as a ransom (*antilutron*)[11] for all men." That is one of the great affirmations of the gospel, and the mention of the ransom price echoes Jesus' own words in Mark 10:45 that the Son of Man

---

10. The apostle identified the one mediator as "the man Christ Jesus." In this context the term *man* (*anthrōpos*) is generic and gives prominence to Christ's humanity. Likely the gnostic teachers denied the reality of the incarnation, but Paul affirmed its reality by stressing that Christ belonged to the category of men.

11. In the phrase "a ransom for all" (*antilutron huper pantōn*) both *anti* ("instead of") and *huper* ("in behalf of") are combined with "ransom" (*lutron*) and indicate that Christ's death was substitutionary. The verb *redeem* (*lutroō*) is used in Titus 2:14: "who [Christ] gave himself for us to redeem us from all wickedness." The idea is that of ransom, the cost of man's redemption. The concept of "ransom" (*lutron*) and its word group retains full force and should not be watered down to mean liberation in a general sense. See George E. Ladd, *A Theology of the New Testament,* pp. 427–434.

came to give "his life as a ransom for many." Ransom money was paid for the freedom of prisoners of war or for the freedom of a slave in the ancient world. The ransom price for our salvation was Christ's life and suffering. What He paid sets us free from the grip of sin. He "gave himself for us to redeem us from all wickedness . . ." (Titus 2:14).

The stress must fall on the cost of man's redemption. To be the Savior of mankind cost Jesus everything. To tell men and women of God's love cost Him His life. To bring them into fellowship with God cost Him pain and sacrifice. Man by his own efforts cannot escape the power of sin, but through the cross Christ paid the price for man's freedom. Indeed anyone who accepts His saving work is free.

4. There is one gospel for all men (2:7). The gospel was proclaimed in the Old Testament, but, according to the divine plan, the full significance of the gospel was not disclosed until Christ offered Himself as a ransom. The cross of Christ stands as a special testimony to the eternal love of God in dealing with the sins of the world.

The apostle Paul was appointed as a herald, an apostle, and a teacher to bear witness of this testimony to the Gentiles. Conscious that God had laid on him so great and hazardous a task, he wrote, "And of this gospel I was appointed a herald and an apostle and a teacher. That is why I am suffering as I am" (2 Tim. 1:11–12).[12] His work among the Gentiles left no doubt that the gospel is for all regardless of their rank, class, or social standing. Since the wonderful news of Christ's redeeming work is for all, we should pray for all, keeping before us the will of God and also the needs and suffering of the world. The gospel teaches us

---

12. The apostle's own evaluation of his suffering was that it was in accord with the will of God (2 Cor. 11:16f.; 12:10; Gal. 6:17; Phil. 3:10f.; 1 Thess. 3:3f.). His suffering is a prominent theme in 2 Timothy. It was necessitated by his vocation as a minister of the gospel (1:11–12). His suffering was done in behalf of the gospel (1:8). It verified that he lived "a godly life in Christ Jesus" (3:12). Paul admonished Timothy to endure suffering as he himself had in the faithful guarding of the gospel (2:1–13). His suffering was tied to the witness that he had borne (2:2–3, 8–10; 3:14–15), and it was done for the sake of the gospel in order that others might receive benefit (2:8–10).

to pray to one God through the one Mediator, "who gave himself a ransom for all. . . ."

III. Order in Worship (2:8-15)

The local church in Ephesus did not have church manuals describing such things as how to conduct worship. The apostle knew that the church is not merely a place of worship, but a community that worships the living God. A church that is spiritually sensitive to the truths of the gospel and ministers and worships to the glory of God can be truly described as ". . . the church of the living God, the pillar and foundation of the truth" (1 Tim. 3:15). Mindful of the importance of proper dignity and order in worship, the apostle dealt with problems in the Ephesian churches.

A. Men and Public Prayer (2:8)

Here men were called upon by Paul to pray.[13] They were to offer prayer everywhere (literally, "in every place"), that is, "throughout the church" or "in every Christian meeting place." Where the meetings were held men were to offer prayer with uplifted hands. Their attention was called to purity of actions and motives, both of which are spiritual conditions for effective prayer.

---

13. The apostle's intent is not to belittle the status of women. Christianity had given them a new status (Gal. 3:28). The cultural factors that denied women active participation in public worship must have been irksome to the church. Society of that day did not approve of women's participation in public assemblies. Women were almost universally regarded as inferior to men. This was particularly true in the entirely male-dominated Jewish world. For the most part the status of the woman was no better in the pagan world, in which there was little understanding of the equality of the sexes. To avoid bringing reproach on the Ephesian church, Paul's advice was that men lead in prayer. The apostle did not mean that women should never take an active part in public worship. Every person was expected to take part in the service (1 Cor. 14:26). Furthermore, "every woman who prays or prophesies with her head uncovered dishonors her head" (11:5). The strong implication is that women may pray publicly. Because of the old ways of a society it is necessary at times for Christians to forego certain liberties and to accept restraints to avoid bringing reproach on the church.

1. Pure actions. Stretching forth holy hands is a particular posture in prayer. This was a common practice among the Jews, but in the New Testament no other reference is made to the practice. As we have noted, prayer is a Christian responsibility but particularly significant is that the uplifted hands are to be "holy" (*hosioi cheires*). Hands symbolize daily conduct, since they are used in most of our activities. If a worshiper soils his hands with forbidden things, his prayers are little more than a formality. He has lived as though he were not a praying man. Hands stained by unworthy deeds must be cleansed before they are lifted up to God in prayer. He who prays in the congregation must raise pure and undefiled hands, hands that have been cleansed.

2. Pure motives. Pure actions are important, but a pure heart is also essential to worship and communion with God. To please God the heart must be right: "without anger or disputing." Our wrath usually works evil toward others, but for prayer to be acceptable it must be free of indignation or resentment. Again and again Christ stressed that we cannot receive forgiveness as long as we have feelings of hostility toward others. His words are especially searching when He says, "and when you stand praying, if you hold anything against anyone, forgive him, so that your Father in heaven may forgive you your sins" (Mark 11:25).

The worshiper must not be given to wrath, but he must be without disputing (*dialogismos*). The Greek word translated as "disputing" can also mean "doubting." Often it is used for quarreling with others, but it can signify disputing with one's self concerning the value of prayer. Disputing is the basic idea, whether it is understood as arguing with others[14] or with one's self. Entertaining hostility toward anyone makes it impossible for us to worship God with a pure heart. Moreover, there should be no question about the value of prayer. Communion with God is to be free of doubts and entered into with confidence that our petitions will be answered.

---

14. The tone of the entire passage seems to indicate that the reference is to disputes that have ethical implication rather than to intellectual doubt.

B. Women and Worship (2:9–15)

The apostle turned to the conduct of Christian women in the worship service. His concern was to curtail any disorders created in worship. Of course these instructions have relevance beyond public worship and can be applied to men as well as women. The rule for both men and women is modesty, decency, and propriety. Appearance and bearing that are fitting for worship are fitting for other occasions.

The key to understanding Paul's view of the women's position in the church is Galatians 3:28: "There is neither . . . male nor female, for you are all one in Christ Jesus." At first glance other statements from Paul may appear to stand in conflict with the principle of equality of women in the church, especially if the cultural and biblical context of such statements is disregarded. A fundamental rule is to interpret Scripture, particularly difficult passages, against its background.

Undoubtedly women in the first-century church did enjoy considerable freedom and equal status with men. At Ephesus some of the women apparently were overreacting to their newfound equality and were prone to abuse their liberty. "The apostle found it necessary to propose certain restraints to maintain decency and order within the community, especially in worship."[15]

1. Women's proper demeanor (2:9–10). Appearance and conduct are important, especially for the worship service.

a. Reserve and sober modesty (2:9). To secure the right spirit in worship Paul recommends modesty in dress. He knew that the manner of dress is a mirror of attitude. Indeed the Christian woman is to dress attractively, but she is not to be ostentatious and offensive in what she wears. She is to strive to be a credit to the Lord in all areas of her life, including that of dress.

Noteworthy are two words used here to describe the proper conduct of Christian women. The first is "decency" (*aidōs*, "shamefacedness, modesty"). The thought is that the Christian is to avoid excess in her personal attire. No particular stereo-

15. Donald Guthrie, *New Testament Theology,* p. 775.

typed style is prescribed, but regardless of style she is to be well-dressed and avoid shabby and repulsive raiment. She must be careful not to transgress the rule of modesty.

The second term is "propriety" (*sōphrosunē*, "discretion, prudence"). As this suggests, a Christian woman is to have a sound frame of mind that exercises self-control. The result is that she is not given to vanity or worldly display. She is discreet in her dress, neither wearing rags with the hope of impressing others with her humility nor arraying herself in extravagant clothing, which may arouse envy in others. New fashions and beautiful clothes are quite proper for the Christian woman as long as they are decent. There is no virtue in looking old-fashioned or threadbare. That can be bad taste and false modesty.

b. Spiritual adornment and good deeds (2:10). The prudent woman dresses simply, but her true adornment is not outward show "with braided hair or gold or pearls or expensive clothes." Of course this does not deny her all outward adornment, but as we are reminded by Donald Guthrie:

> The plaiting of the hair was a usual feature of Jewish women's hairstyle, and in the more elaborate types the plaits were fastened with ribbons and bows. . . . Such tendencies to ostentatious adornment must be resisted by Christian women, and the same applies to the use of jewelry and costly clothing. In all these injunctions the one dominating idea is the avoidance of anything designed merely to promote ostentation, with all its accompanying dangers.[16]

The Christian woman is to adorn herself with good deeds. That is sufficient. She need not get caught up in the cult of beauty. The greatest asset is her godly life, and her true beauty is in good works, which are "a life of selfless devotion to others." Good works are proper and natural for any God-fearing person. They reveal the real motives and the spiritual quality of life.

2. Women's proper sphere (2:11–15). Certain women with a new sense of freedom were tempted to go too far. They were dictatorial and created confusion in the church.

a. Self-restraint (2:11–12). In urging them to exercise restraint, did Paul disqualify women from teaching and leadership roles

---

16. *The Pastoral Epistles,* (Tyndale New Testament Commentaries), p. 75.

in the church? Many scholars have concluded that he did and they rightly note that he did say, "A woman should learn in quietness and full submission. I do not permit a woman to teach or to have authority over a man; she must be silent." Before deciding, we should take into consideration two facts.

First, the teachings and practices of both Jesus and Paul are the norm. Any apparent exceptions, such as 1 Timothy 2:11–12 and 1 Corinthians 14:34–35, are due to circumstances that existed in particular local churches.

Jesus did not teach or do anything that would indicate disapproval of women assuming leadership roles, nor did He treat women as inferiors. Among His disciples were several women (Luke 8:2).[17] They were learning from their Lord and were ministering to Him. His conversation with the Samaritan certainly did not square with the rules of convention of that day (John 4:1–42). Jesus rejected the stereotype of the woman in the kitchen when He praised Mary for listening to His teaching instead of helping Martha with her household duties (Luke 10:38–42). After Jesus' resurrection, He appeared first to Mary Magdalene. Since she was a woman, her testimony would not have been acceptable in a court of law. Yet Jesus sent her to bear witness to the resurrection (Matt. 28:1–10).

Following Jesus' example, the apostle Paul had the same perspective. According to him, everyone in public worship had something to contribute: "... a hymn, or a word of instruction, a revelation, a tongue, or an interpretation. .... For you can all prophesy in turn so that everyone may be instructed and encouraged" (1 Cor. 14:26, 31). The only reason Paul urged Christian women to be silent was to maintain order and decency within public worship (1 Cor. 14:34f.; 1 Tim. 2:11–12).

It is clear that Paul understood that women would exercise leadership roles in the church. By no means in 1 Timothy 2:11–12 and 1 Corinthians 14:34–35 did Paul intend to enunciate a principle that could apply in all contexts. Without any reluctance he assumed that women would pray and speak publicly, but at the

---

17. The fact that a woman was not one of the Twelve could have been due to precautions against rumors of scandal.

same time he was concerned that they wear their veils to avoid transgressing social conventions and bringing reproach on the church (1 Cor. 11:5).

There is little doubt that the Spirit bestows on women gifts for ministry in the church. Surely these could include the gift of leadership, the gift of teaching, and the gift of prophecy.[18] To say the least, this squares with God's promise of the Holy Spirit for all flesh and with the fact that both men and women might be given prophetic and other spiritual gifts (Acts 2:17). The Holy Spirit, who is sovereign in the distribution of the gifts, has never limited His gifts to men (1 Cor. 12:11).

Second, a proper understanding of 1 Timothy 2:11–12 must also take into consideration Paul's intent in the Pastoral Epistles. A number of times Paul urged Timothy to keep "the pattern of sound doctrine" and to guard the truth entrusted to him by the Holy Spirit (2 Tim. 1:13–14). He warned his young friend of the danger of false teachers and to be especially watchful. His purpose was to warn against unorthodox teachings and to provide guidance for the local church.

2 Timothy 3:6–7 reflects that heretical teachings had influenced certain women at Ephesus. "They [false teachers] are the

---

18. The gospel does not obliterate sexual distinctions and roles that women are more fitted for in society, but it has been in the vanguard in liberating women from an inferior status and giving dignity to womanhood. The following exposition of 1 Corinthians 11:2–16 makes this clear: "(1) A woman leading congregational worship must preserve her sexual identity as a woman. As a woman, she will dress in a manner different from that of a man; and the man is reminded that he too should maintain this differentiation. The nature of these differences will be dictated by what seems proper to the group concerned. 'Judge for yourselves,' the Apostle advises, thus laying the situation open for divergent opinions. The application may vary, but the principle is to be adhered to—men and women are different because God has made them so, and being 'one in Christ' does not obliterate this difference. (2) A woman leading congregational worship does so by virtue of her relationship to Christ, not by virtue of her relationship to a man. She does not stand before the congregation as representative of her role in the created order, as the glory of a man, but rather as representative of her role in the redemptive order, in the image of God. In covering her hair and shoulders, the woman demonstrates to the congregation that now in Christ she is restored to the original dignity and equality intended by God when he created 'man' male and female. No longer in subjection to man, she stands before the congregation in relation to God, as does the male. Thus the veil symbolizes her 'authority' (verse 10) to stand and speak as man's equal before God." Donald A. Hagner and Murray J. Harris, eds., *Pauline Studies*, p. 45.

kind who worm their way into homes and gain control over weak-willed women, who are loaded down with sins and are swayed by all kinds of evil desires, always learning but never able to acknowledge the truth." Here a feminine word (*gunaikaria*) is used for "weak-willed women," but what is significant is that those guilty of teaching false doctrine are referred to in verse 2 by a generic term—"For men (*anthrōpoi*) will be lovers of themselves" (KJV).[19] As in English, the Greek term *men* is broad enough to include men and women.[20] Does this not indicate that at Ephesus women were involved in learning and in disseminating unorthodox teachings? These women were allowed to attend the church services and even to teach others. Likely the men in the congregation were disturbed at these women's silly and destructive ideas and felt that they should be disciplined. They needed to learn, as others did, the truth of the gospel and to stop trying to lord it over men. Their failure to grasp Christian truth and maintain a biblical balance must have been the reason Paul urged Christian women at Ephesus to learn in silence, to submit to the constituted authority in the church, and to refrain from teaching[21] and exercising authority over a man. Paul refused to tolerate anything that would reduce Christian worship to disorder. Since certain women were creating disorder in worship, it is understandable that he would urge them to be silent.

It comes as no surprise that Paul unreservedly recognized the leadership and ministry exercised by women in the Christian community. Women were spoken of as his fellow workers (Phil.

---

19. The apostle's words in 2 Timothy 3:1–5 applied to his day as well as ours. The phrase "in the last day" may seem to refer to a future period but it was the conviction of the New Testament writers that the new age began with the first coming of Jesus Christ and that the last days had dawned. Accordingly Peter, on the day of Pentecost, quoted Joel's prophecy that "in the last days" God would pour out his Spirit on all people and that promise was now fulfilled. Thus Paul, as well as we, lived in the last days. What he described in 2 Timothy 3 was present in his day and related particularly to the ministry of Timothy at Ephesus.

20. The New International Version affirms the generic meaning of *anthrōpoi* in verse 2 by translating it as "people."

21. Paul wrote in the present active indicative. Therefore he did not say, "I will never permit a woman to teach" but rather, "I am not permitting a woman to teach."

4:3). Phoebe was described as a deacon[22] of the church at Cenchrea and was given the same honor as a man in a similar ministry (Rom. 16:1). Priscilla worked alongside of her husband in the ministry (Acts 18:26; Rom. 16:3). Tryphena and Tryphosa were singled out by Paul as "those women who work hard in the Lord" (Rom. 16:12). There is no hint that women were involved in any other ministry than what is basic to the work of the church.

b. Adam and Eve (2:13–14). Something was happening at Ephesus that deeply concerned Paul. As we have already noted, unorthodox beliefs were being taught in the church. Among the false teachers there probably were women who were teaching "false doctrines" and were devoting themselves to "myths and endless genealogies" (1:4). Because the women did not have a grasp of the truth, Paul admonished them to be silent. In his appeal to the first chapter of Genesis he observed the priority of Adam in creation—"Adam was formed first"—and the priority of Eve in sin—"the woman . . . was deceived and became a sinner."

The events in Ephesus were reminiscent of the situation in Eden. Eve had been deceived into believing erroneous teachings. Satan enticed her with the prospect of knowledge that God supposedly had withheld, and she touched the tree of good and evil, thinking that she would become like God. Then she shared with Adam the unorthodox teachings. Both ate of the forbidden fruit. The aftermath of what they did was fatal. They were enslaved by sin and death; the happy relationship between God and man was broken; the curse of sin fell upon all.

Something similar to that could have happened at Ephesus. The church there could have been destroyed as Adam and Eve destroyed themselves. To avoid this Paul wanted to restrain the women at Ephesus from teaching until they were well instructed in the faith.

c. Saved through childbearing (2:15). The Greek reads "the childbearing," which probably refers to the most significant birth

---

22. The word *deacon* (*diakonos*) is the same word used to describe Epaphras (Col. 1:7), Paul (Col. 1:25), and Tychicus (Col. 4:7). The word can be translated as "minister." The use of the same designation for Phoebe suggests that she exercised authority in the church.

of all—the birth of Jesus Christ.[23] Through Eve transgression entered this world, but it was through another woman, Mary, that salvation came. Through the act of childbirth the Savior came into the world. So women will be saved through the incarnate Son "if they continue in faith, love and holiness. . . ."

Like Eve, the women at Ephesus were easily led astray. Their need was proper instruction in the faith. They were to learn in submission to the church leaders and not seek to teach until they had an accurate grasp of Christian truth. The gospel always fosters liberation, and indeed has elevated and dignified womanhood.

IV. Conclusion

Worship is our response to God's presence with us and in us. The indwelling Holy Spirit is the spring and source of worship. God comes to us through the Holy Spirit and touches our lives, and our response is to be worship that centers in devotion to Jesus and finds expression in thanksgiving, praise, adoration, and prayer to God. Such worship has spiritual vitality. It influences all concerns of life.

As Paul made clear, prayer is a significant element of worship. God is the author of prayer. The Holy Spirit himself moves us to supplication, to intercession, to thanksgiving. But prayer is never an automatic thing, and for many it is an exceptional thing. So many things crowd out or kill our prayer life. Worldly attitudes— worrying about money and about getting ahead in our business or profession—can consume us. Dissensions with our colleagues and in the church hinder us in our devotions. Undoubtedly tensions and frustrations are often symptoms of our spiritual decadence. Many things of the world fill our lives, but when there is room in our hearts for His active presence, the Holy Spirit prays in us (Rom. 8:26).

Absolute priority should be given to earnest prayer both private and corporate, but without discipline that is impossible.

---

23. Guthrie, *The Pastoral Epistles*, (Tyndale New Testament Commentaries), p. 78, understands the article to refer to the whole process of childbearing rather than to a particular birth. The interpretations of verse 15 are various.

Spiritual discipline is a vital side of discipleship, and it sets us free to pray or, to put it another way, for the Holy Spirit to pray through us. The discipline of prayer prevents the world from consuming us and makes us sensitive to the voice of God and to the needs of the church and world.

Paul's perspective on prayer no doubt was right. He understood that all circumstances and all people can be brought within the scope of our prayers. After all, it is God's desire that we "live peaceful and quiet lives in all godliness and holiness" and that "all men . . . be saved and . . . come to a knowledge of the truth." Communion with God can have a decisive impact on the affairs of the world. And, too, through our prayers the one God works to bring men and women to faith in the "one mediator . . . , the man Christ Jesus, who gave himself as a ransom for all men." Persistent prayer has removed more obstacles that stood in the way of faith in Christ and Christian growth than we will ever know in this life. The resources of heaven and the provisions of Calvary have been made available to so many through the prayers of God's people.

Genuine heartfelt prayer is basic to vitality in worship. Another element of worship is order. That is the kind of order in which modesty, moderation, and good taste are the rule for both men and women. That is the kind of order that is conducive to the teaching and proclamation of the gospel. Paul's injunctions about maintaining good order in the church still apply, but our situation may appear to be quite different from that of the Pauline churches. In the church at Ephesus were women who were sowing seeds of discord and heretical doctrine. But we still have those kinds of people in the church— people who go off on a tangent, people who fail to hold to Christian doctrine, people who refuse to submit to the authority of Scripture and to those who are over them in the Lord.

No one, whether male or female, who manifests these tendencies should have the opportunity to exercise a teaching or a preaching ministry in the church. Teachings contrary to cardinal doctrines of the faith disrupt the life of the local church and can throw it into a crisis and destroy it. In the interest of preserving the worship of God and proper order in the church, heretical teachings should not be tolerated in the congregation of the redeemed.

5

Standards for Leadership

(3:1–13)

Building up other people in the faith is an important part of Christian leadership. This is true of Christian leadership at all levels, especially in the local church. Never can the leader's capabilities and competence be divorced from the kind of Christian he is.

Paul clearly expected all Christians to conduct themselves in such fashion that their lives were consistent with the life and teaching of Christ. The leaders of the churches were to see that this level of life was maintained by discipline and Christian teaching. Laxity in living the Christian life, beyond a certain point, was not to be tolerated (1 Cor. .5:1–13; 10:1–12, 14–22; 11:17–24). Living in conformity with the demands of Christ is the very foundation of the healthy Christian life.

The pressures, values, and practices of a secular society have threatened to erode the Christian life. The world seeks to press the church into its own mold. No doubt this was the reason Paul emphasized the Christian life and knowledge of the gospel as essential for leadership in the church. Above all, ministerial leaders need to reflect in their lives practices and traits compatible with the gospel. By example and precept they are to provide direction for the church in a pagan culture and to foster commitment to the Christian life among the believers.

The qualifications advocated by Paul for ministerial leadership are part of God's holy Word and are applicable to the church and its leaders in every generation.

I. Leadership in the Local Church

According to Paul, an isolated, individualistic Christian is abnormal. The normal Christian life is expressed in a fellowship of worship, caring, and sharing, under the authoritative guidance of the leaders of the community. The local church is not based on a cult of personalities; nevertheless, its leaders are important to the Christian fellowship. Their task is to keep the church faithful to the gospel.

A. The Church Leaders

Three of the terms used in the New Testament to designate ministerial leaders seem to call for special notice. The first is "overseer" (*episkopos*), which has been rendered in a number of English versions as "bishop."[1] The word refers to one who has the responsibility of caring for or overseeing and thus literally means "overseer" or "superintendent."

At Miletus, Paul sent to Ephesus for the elders and reminded them that the Holy Spirit had made them overseers (*episkopoi*, Acts 20:17). Moreover, he admonished the overseers to "be shepherds of the church of God" (Acts 20:28). This helps us to understand the duties of the overseers. Like a shepherd of a flock, they were to exercise loving care and concern for the people of God. Their supreme example was Jesus Christ who because of His selfless service is described as "the Shepherd and Overseer of your souls" (1 Peter 2:25).

The men who were called overseers were responsible for the care of the local churches. Both 1 Timothy 3:1 and Titus 1:7 make reference to an overseer (singular). Neither of these suggests that there was only one leader per church. Acts 20:28 and Philippians 1:1 suggest several overseers were at work in a single local church. In New Testament times the authority of the overseer (bishop) was limited to a local church, and he seems to have been a member of a group that exercised leadership in the

---

1. See King James Version, Revised Standard Version, Phillips, and New English Bible.

congregation. However, in modern times a bishop exercises authority over several churches and pastors.

A second New Testament designation for church leaders is that of "elder" (*presbuteros*). The first time that we hear of elders is when Moses appointed them to assist in advising and caring for the people (Num. 11:26). They were guardians and representatives of the Jewish community both in exile (Jer. 24:1) and in the homeland (Ezek. 8:1f.). The Jewish synagogue had elders whose function was to lead in worship and exercise discipline.

Does the New Testament make a distinction between elders and overseers? In Acts 20:17, 28 and Titus 1:5-7 the words *elder* and *overseer* are identified as pertaining to the same persons. A comparison of 1 Timothy 3:2-7, which sets forth the qualifications of the "overseer," with Titus 1:6-9, which specifies the qualification of the elder, discloses that they are more or less the same. The terms *elder* and *overseer* were used interchangeably to describe the same leaders, but one described the leader personally and the other his function. The elders were the respected and older men in the congregation. As leaders their function (like that of a shepherd) was to exercise oversight, guarding the faith, maintaining the life of the church, and promoting its work.

A third word employed to describe ministerial leaders is "deacon" (*diakonos*). It occurs frequently in the New Testament and means "a servant, one who ministers." The ministry of deacons can be traced back to the Jerusalem church (Acts 6:1-6).[2] Seven men were chosen by that church "to wait on tables" so that the apostles could devote themselves to "the ministry (*diakonia*) of the word." The deacons' work was mainly practical, and they devoted themselves to caring for the poor in the church and to other matters that pertained to administration.

It should not be overlooked that these leaders had spiritual functions as well. The first deacons were expected to possess charismatic

---

2. Traditionally the seven chosen in Acts 6:1-6 have been described as "deacons," but the word *deacon* does not occur in this passage. The author does employ *diakoneō* ("to wait on," v. 2) and *diakonia* ("daily distribution," v. 1; "ministry," v. 4) in these verses. Both of these belong to the same word group as "deacon."

qualities—"full of the Spirit and wisdom" (Acts 6:3). The charismatic ministry of two of the deacons is noted in the Book of Acts. Stephen had a notable preaching ministry, which was confirmed by mighty signs and wonders (Acts 6:8). Philip also was active in the missionary enterprise (8:4–40). So their service was by no means confined to the material interests of the church.

The apostle Paul saw himself as a servant (*diakonos*) and expressed this fact in varying ways: a servant of the gospel (Eph. 3:7), a servant through whom the Christians in Corinth had come to faith (2 Cor. 6:4), a servant of Christ (11:23), a servant of the church (Col. 1:25). As a servant of the gospel Paul, like his Lord, was concerned about man's physical and spiritual well-being. On behalf of Christ he traveled far and wide to preach the gospel, but he also raised money in gentile churches to relieve the distress of the poor Christians in Jerusalem (2 Cor. 8, 9).

Whatever work was done in the early church could be called "services" or "ministries" (1 Cor. 12:5), and those who performed ministerial tasks were deacons (*diakonoi*) in a sense. However, it was not too long before the service of the deacons became distinct from that of overseer or elder (Phil. 1:1; 1 Tim. 3:8–13), and the work of the deacons developed into a special office[3] that made them responsible for the material concerns of the Christian community. But like the overseers, they were required to be morally and spiritually qualified for their task.

The structure of the early church was conducive to great diversity in ministries. The elders (overseers) could be seen to correspond somewhat to modern-day pastors.[4] Deacons must have served under the elders and were real "helps" to them (1 Cor. 12:28). Rather soon after New Testament times there emerged three prominent orders of ministry: bishops, pastors (priests), and deacons.

---

3. Colin Brown, ed., *The New International Dictionary of New Testament Theology,* p. 558.

4. The Presbyterians make a distinction between the teaching elder (the pastor) and the ruling elders. The latter's responsibilities fall in the area of discipline and the spiritual welfare of the congregation. The biblical basis for this distinction is 1 Timothy 5:17: "The elders who direct the affairs of the church well are worthy of double honor, especially those whose work is preaching and teaching."

B. The Ambition for Greater Usefulness (3:1)

An appeal is made to a trustworthy saying—"If anyone sets his heart on being an overseer, he desires a noble task." This could have been something of a proverb. The intent is to exalt Christian leadership. The aspiration to leadership is an honorable ambition. Anyone aspiring to leadership in the church should be cautious about carnal ambition. The motivation for seeking leadership responsibilities may be to satisfy selfish desires.

A person who aspires to become a leader (*episcopē*, "overseer") may be seeking power and preeminence among Christians, but that does not change the fact that he seeks an honorable and noble work. Motives for leadership may be mixed. Carnal means may be used to secure a position. In itself the desire for leadership in the church is good and noble. Why? The office of the overseer is good, and his task is noble. No one should belittle Christian leadership, because the work is honorable. Any person with ambition for greater usefulness and with pure motives is to be commended for aspiring to Christian leadership. Whenever a premium is placed on spiritual values, there is high estimate of the Christian ministry. Indeed it is a noble task.

II. Qualities of an Overseer (3:2-7)

The vital qualifications of the overseer (pastor/minister) are described, but nothing is said about his duties. Many of the early Christians came from backgrounds where moral vices were the rule rather than the exception. While there may be other qualifications, the Christian life is still the prime essential for the one chosen to serve as a leader in the church.

A. Personal Life (3:2-3)

The Christian leader's reputation is vital to his usefulness and success in the ministry. His life must be ordered so that he has a good reputation among the church members and a good report

77

in the community. To use Paul's expression, he "must[5] be above reproach." The word (*anepilēmpton*) means literally "not to be taken hold of." To be above reproach, the minister must offer nothing that can be taken hold of and used legitimately to call in question his character. Should accusations be made against him, an investigation would disprove the charges. He is, therefore, to be blameless or irreproachable. What are the particular areas in which the Christian leader should be above reproach?

1. Marital status. The minister should be "the husband of but one wife." Literally the Greek reads simply "a one-woman man" or "a one-wife man." Standing at the beginning of the list, the phrase gives prominence to the importance of the marriage relationship. But exactly what did Paul have in mind? One wife at a time or one during a lifetime? Obviously, the phrase "the husband of but one wife" can be understood in a number of ways. Its meaning has been debated from ancient times to the present.

Noteworthy are a few of the interpretations that have been advocated. First, the Christian leader must have a wife. If this were true, an unmarried person would be ineligible. What about Paul? Was he married? The possibility cannot be categorically ruled out, but as far as we know, he was not. However, it is clear that he was an elder. He reminded Timothy to stir up the gift that he had received by the laying on of the hands of the presbytery, that is, the body of elders (1 Tim. 4:14). Later Timothy was urged to stir up the gift of God that he had received by Paul's laying his hands on him (2 Tim. 1:6). Therefore, the apostle must have been a member of a presbytery and thus an elder. It is quite unlikely that he intended to exclude bachelors on the basis of their marital status. That interpretation is contrary to

---

5. The Greek that is rendered "must" (*dei*) in verses 2 and 7 literally means "it is necessary." In biblical usage the term stands for the will of a personal God and expresses the will of God as claiming man in every situation in life and as giving direction to life on the basis of its saving purpose. Paul's use of *dei* is no exception to this (Rom. 8:26; 12:3; 1 Cor. 8:2; 2 Cor. 2:3; 11:30; 12:1; 1 Tim. 3:15; 5:13; 2 Tim. 2:6; Titus 1:7, 11).

the entire passage, which stresses the character of the overseer rather than his status.[6]

Second, the Christian leader whose wife has died must not remarry. He must marry once but never again. The facts militate against this view, which assumes that a stigma is attached to remarriage after the death of a spouse. Neither the Old Testament nor the New Testament forbids widows to remarry. Widows desiring to be supported by the church were to remain single (1 Tim. 5:9). On the other hand, young widows were advised to remarry (5:14). Nowhere does Scripture prohibit a second marriage after the death of the first spouse. Death cancels the marriage contract (Rom. 7:3), leaving the surviving partner free to marry again.

Third, the Christian leader must be an example of marital faithfulness. The bulk of the members of the first-century church came out of paganism, in which moral vices and sexual excesses were commonplace. There is no reason to think that the background of the Ephesian converts was any different. The qualification "the husband of but one wife" does not necessarily mean that the Christian leader had never sinned in this area, but that he had been changed by the transforming grace of Christ so that he now was faithful to his one wife.[7]

Such marital fidelity involves more than the legal aspect—not guilty of the act of adultery. In the eyes of the law there may be no question that the Christian leader is a one-woman man, but his actions and attitudes toward his wife may demonstrate that he is not truly a one-woman man. "The Old Testament prohibition of adultery is not confined to the negative avoidance of the sinful act. It finds true fulfillment only in the love of spouses who are joined together by God (Rom. 13:9)."[8] The positive

---

6. The false teachers had a low view of marriage (1 Tim. 4:3). To counter their prohibition against marrying Paul could have urged the overseers and deacons to marry. As he wrote, "everything God created is good" (4:4).

7. The Word of God consistently describes the evils of immorality and divorce as sin. An urgent need in present-day churches is the exercise of more discipline in these areas. However, it should never be forgotten that these sins can be forgiven through genuine repentance and that individuals can be purified of such sinful inclinations through the indwelling Spirit of holiness.

8. Gerhard Kittel, ed., *Theological Dictionary of the New Testament*, vol. 4, p. 734.

emphasis is evident in Homer A. Kent's explanation of the qualification when he says, "The phrase by Paul is stated positively.
The overseer must be a one-woman man. He must be devoted
to her and give her all the love and consideration that a wife
deserves."[9]

2. *"Temperate."* The King James Version renders the word
nēphalios as "vigilant," suggesting being "watchful" or "cir-
cumspect"; but here it should be taken as "temperate" in its
broad sense, especially since drunkenness is forbidden in verse
3. The word refers to the pursuit of pleasure. There are matters
more vital to the Christian leader than pleasures. This does not
deny that there are pleasures for him. By God's help he is a
master of himself. Such a person is moderate and well-balanced.
Therefore, he is able to exercise restraint in the pursuit of carnal
pleasures. Spiritual concern and sincerity give him a proper
estimate of what is vital and lasting.

3. *"Self-controlled."* The fundamental idea is that the overseer
is "sensible" (*sōphrōn*) or has a sound mind. He indeed is
prudent and self-controlled (cf. 2 Tim. 1:7; Titus 1:8; 2:2, 5). Being
thoughtful and levelheaded, he is grounded in faith. Here the
words of Romans 12:3 are apt: "For by the grace given me I say
to every one of you: Do not think of yourself more highly than
you ought, but rather think of yourself with sober judgment, in
accordance with the measure of faith God has given you."

Prudence is a matter of attitude and an aspect of love in
which a balance is maintained between commitment and dis-
tance. Neither impulsive desires nor a haughty spirit controls
the prudent Christian leader. At times he may be tempted to
throw restraint to the winds and become conceited. However,
he maintains respect for his own strengths and weaknesses, for
others, and for the particular situation that may involve problems and spiritual and intellectual temptations. His soundness
of mind is due not to his own moral achievement and good
works but to the renewing of his mind by the Holy Spirit and his
receiving "a measure of faith"—spiritual gifts for ministry. God's

---

9. *The Pastoral Epistles*, p. 130.

blessings provide the impetus for balanced living and level-headedness.

4. *"Respectable."* The Greek word (*kosmios*) means "orderly" and implies a well-ordered life with emphasis on good behavior. The inner life renewed and sanctified by the Holy Spirit is normally in good order and serves as a spring for outward conduct. Confusion within prompts disorder in behavior, but harmony within gives rise to an orderly lifestyle. Such a meaningful pattern in the leader's daily activity is vital. When people observe him, they will see what is attractive and honorable. They will see God's power in his life and living.

5. *"Hospitable."* Few provisions were made for those who traveled in the first-century world. There were no motels or hotels, only a few inns, poorly equipped and often places of vice. Many of the early Christians traveled frequently for evangelistic and other purposes. The Christian leader was to be an example of a believer who opened his home to the traveling preachers and teachers and to those who were homeless due to persecution or poverty.

Our situation is different. The provisions for travelers today are more than ample. But it is well to remember that Christians belong to one family and that it may be nothing more than feelings of selfishness and inadequacy that crimp our expressions of hospitality.

6. *Aptitude for teaching.* A Christian leader should be an apt teacher (*didaktikos*), that is, have the competence to teach others. Evidently a distinction was made between the Christian leaders who had ability in teaching and those who did not. In 1 Timothy 5:17 (KJV), the elders that "labour in the word and doctrine" (preach) are singled out for special consideration. This implies that there were those among the elders who performed various duties and exercised oversight in matters of discipline while a special group had a preaching and teaching ministry. All the elders took part in guiding the church, but some of them had the facility and responsibility for rightly dividing the Word and instructing the flock in the faith. Today these are called pastors (clergy).

The pastoral ministry is essentially a teaching ministry (Titus 1:9). There is an increasing need for ministers to have an aptitude for teaching, especially as the standards of education rise. Christians grow and mature in Christ as they are rooted and grounded in the Word of God. The preaching of the gospel may be primarily intended to convince, rebuke, or exhort, but it must be a doctrinal ministry, an exposition of the Word of God. It was precisely an expository preaching ministry that Paul had in Ephesus. For three years he labored in that city in Word and doctrine. In his farewell to the elders of the church he declared, "For I have not hesitated to proclaim to you the whole will of God ... but have taught you publicly and from house to house" (Acts 20:27, 20). Every minister should do likewise. An intelligent presentation of the gospel requires skill in teaching. This makes a theological education biblical.

7. *Not a winebibber.* The phrase literally means "one should not sit long at his wine." The Christian leader must not indulge in the use of alcohol. Addiction to strong drink makes him unworthy of whatever position he has in the church. Of course Timothy was exhorted to take a little wine as medicine (1 Tim. 5:23), but in our culture abstinence for the sake of the gospel is the best practice. "It is better not to eat meat or drink wine or to do anything else that will cause your brother to fall" (Rom. 14:21).

8. *"Not violent but gentle."* The word *violent* (*plēktēs*) signifies a giver of blows. No Christian should be given to striking others verbally or physically. Our example is the Lord. When He was stricken, He did not strike back.

Such a disposition is desirable, especially in the church leader. He must not be a belligerent spitfire or quick-tempered, but gentle (*epieikēs*), manifesting the noble qualities of forebearance, fairness, and reasonableness. This does not require the leader to compromise the truth, but it does contribute much toward making him an effective representative of His Lord.

9. *"Not quarrelsome."* The literal meaning is "not a fighter" (*amachos*). The Christian leader needs to be conciliatory. The false teachers at Ephesus did not measure up to this require-ment. Being inclined to fight, they devoted themselves to subtle

interpretations of myths and genealogies and promoted "controversies rather than God's work" (1 Tim. 1:4). In contrast, the real Christian leader avoids being contentious, cantankerous, and difficult to get along with. He desires and works toward peace with his fellow man.

10. "Not a lover of money." The Christian leader must be free from loving mammon, even if he does not have much of it. His foremost desire is not to lay up treasures on the earth. He knows that ultimate values are not in rolling in riches and living in affluence and is careful, therefore, to avoid what happened to Demas (2 Tim. 4:10). At the time Paul wrote to the Colossian congregation, Demas was with him (Col. 4:14). But something went wrong, and Demas came to love this present world more than doing God's will. The same can happen to any Christian. Satan is delighted when those who are leaders and zealous for the Christian cause become lukewarm and turn to worldly pursuits.

B. Family Management (3:4–5)

The skill of establishing a Christian home is crucial to leadership in the church. A Christian leader can render no greater service than to lead his family into the richness of the Christian life and to maintain a home that is truly Christian.

Two specifics are singled out.

1. Maintaining good discipline. No man can manage his home well without discipline. There is no biblical support for the modern practice of letting children do as they please. It is also true that bullying in order to keep them in line has no place in good discipline. Fathers are instructed not to provoke their children lest they become discouraged (Eph. 6:4; Col. 3:21). The Christian leader should be an example. In his home he is to exercise his authority so that his children show him "proper respect" (*semnotēs,* "dignity, stateliness"). This suggests that family discipline is to be firm but carried out with complete dignity so that respect for the children is maintained. Such discipline is built on love. This should also be the basis for discipline in the church.

83

2. *An essential qualification.* The Christian leader is to be the priest in his home and is thus responsible for the training and nurture of his wife and children in Christian doctrine and life. His failure to provide spiritual guidance and to exercise proper discipline in his home disqualifies him for leadership in the church. Obviously, the person who does not discharge his family responsibilities is not a good model for the larger family of God. His effectiveness as a spiritual leader in the home reflects how he relates himself to the household of faith and to the members of the congregation. Being a good husband and father is vital to leadership in the church.

C. Spiritual Development (3:6)

It is conceivable that a person could meet all the requirements mentioned and still be disqualified from leadership in the church because of a lack of experience. The Christian leader is not to be a recent convert (*neophutos*, "neophyte, a beginner"). The point, of course, is that length of experience matters more than age.

1. *Significance of maturity.* The literal meaning of the designation "recent convert" (*neophutos*) is "a young plant." A recent convert is one who is newly planted in the faith and lacks the experience and spiritual maturity to provide the leadership needed in the local congregation. Those who are spiritually mature are to be looked to for leadership, but not the beginners, those who have not shown evidence of being rooted and grounded in Christian truth and have not demonstrated maturity in the things of God.

2. *Danger of too-rapid promotion.* Why should a promising new convert not be given a position of prominence in the church? The reason is that he could easily be tempted to become inflated with his own importance. The verb translated as "become conceited" (*tuphoō*) means "wrapped up in smoke." Elevated too quickly, a recent convert can become beclouded with conceit and live behind such a smokescreen of pride that the results are spiritual disaster.

Paul warned of the judgment that fell upon the devil for the sin of pride.[10] The same judgment can be meted out to a recent convert who has been lured into the grip of pride and has put his foolish wisdom against God's truth. He merits the sentence of condemnation that was pronounced upon the devil. To prevent this, the church must have mature leadership. Pride is a great pitfall to church leaders and leads to disaster—the condemnation the devil merited.

D. Reputation Before the Unsaved (3:7)

A good standing in the community is to be desired and cultivated by every Christian. The influence of the local church and especially the influence of its leadership is crucial to the church's evangelistic outreach. The behavior of the Christian leader must command the respect of "outsiders," that is, "unbelievers" (1 Thess. 4:12; Col. 4:5). Otherwise two inevitable results follow.

1. The leader will fall into disgrace. There is no denying that a Christian leader may become the target of unbelievers' hostile criticism because of their hatred of Christ (Rom. 15:3). Generally unbelievers respect Christian ideals, but they are the first to condemn the Christian, particularly the leader or minister, whose life does not measure up to the high ideals of the gospel. Any leader whose personal integrity is open to question will lose the confidence of the community and the church. His lot will be reproach and disgrace rather than appreciation and admiration.

2. The leader will fall into the devil's trap. Likely this refers to the consequence of spiritual deterioration. Guilty of misconduct, the Christian leader brings reproach on the church and himself. But also he falls into the trap set by the devil.[11] Such a one is under the power of the archenemy of God.

---

10. The phrase *judgment of the devil* can be understood to refer to "condemnation wrought by the devil" (subjective genitive). It probably does not signify the condemnation that the devil brings when he lures a person into the grip of pride but rather to the judgment that was pronounced upon the devil for his sin of pride (objective genitive). It is more scriptural to tnink of the devil being condemned (Gen. 3:15; John 12:31; Rom. 16:20) than the devil pronouncing a sentence of condemnation.

11. Here the genitive in the phrase *trap of the devil (pagida tou diabolou)* is subjective ("the trap made by the devil") rather than the objective genitive (the condemnation that fell on the devil for sin).

II. Qualities of Deacons (3:8-10, 12-13)[12]

The function of deacons was that of serving or ministering. What that specifically involved is not described by Paul here. As already noted, among the Seven selected in Acts 6 were those who had charismatic ministries, but it was not too long before the deacons became primarily responsible for the administrative, financial, and business aspects of the church. The qualifications for deacon and overseer are similar. Only the significant variations will be discussed.

A. Spiritual Conviction and Character (3:9-10)

Commitment to sound doctrine produces a sterling character. What a Christian leader believes about God, Christ, the Spirit, the church, and the Christian life is in no way incidental to his lifestyle and ministry. Consider, therefore, what Paul said about this.

1. A firm grasp of the mystery of faith. Leadership in the church demands more than practical skills; it also requires a spiritually perceptive understanding of the faith. The phrase *the mystery of faith* indicates that Paul never ceased to be amazed about God's revelation in Jesus Christ. Indeed God's saving work in Christ is a mystery in that it is to be marveled at. It is a mystery that had been hidden in the long ages of the past and that was promised in Old Testament prophecy but made known fully

---

12. Verse 11 consists of some requirements for women. Commentators are divided as to whether these women were wives of deacons or all adult women of the church or deaconesses. Since the requirements for women stand between the discussion of the qualifications for overseer and for deacon, they must have been servants of the church and had important ministries. While it is difficult to establish precisely the functions of the women mentioned in verse 11, Ephesians 4:11–16 speaks of the living Christ who provides equipping ministries to prepare all the believers for ministry. The women referred to in 1 Timothy 3 must have had special ministries, especially since they were expected, as were the overseers and deacons, to meet certain qualifications: respectable, temperate, and trustworthy. These qualifications have been discussed, but one qualification does not appear either in the list for the overseers or deacons: "not malicious talkers." The word here rendered as "malicious talkers" is the same word for "devil" (*diabolos*, "a slanderer"). Being the greatest slanderer, the devil slanders God and His people, but none of God's servants are to be guilty of carrying tales and disseminating slander.

through Jesus Christ (Rom. 16:25-26). The Word became flesh. God's plan of salvation is a revealed mystery that still provokes wonder and leaves us speechless before its unfathomable depth (Rom. 11:33-36). The Christian leader is to keep a firm hold on the wonderful truths of the gospel.

However, God's revelation in Christ is to be more than abstract truth. The ministerial leader is to hold it "with a clear [*katharos*, "clean"] conscience." The stress falls on sincerity, honesty. Believing what is professed is significant for church leadership. The devoutness of a leader who lacks real convictions about the body of Christian doctrine is a mask to give him credit with others. A sincere acceptance of the cardinal truths of the faith will genuinely shape and fashion the daily life of any Christian. He will live in light of the truth. He will have a pure conscience— a conscience that is guided by the Holy Spirit and does not condemn, because he has a pure life. Sound doctrine produces a sound spiritual life.

2. A tested character. No beginner should occupy a position of leadership (overseer/deacon) in the church. He "must first be tested." The point is that he has to prove himself worthy of the position. To do that he must undergo the careful examination carried out by the believers in the local church. As a Christian he must be above reproach, having lived an exemplary life. Under observation his life must measure up to constant testing in the eyes of the church. Only when the church is assured of his moral and spiritual fitness is he to be considered worthy (assuming that he has met the other requirements) to serve as a leader among the people of God.

B. Present Rewards (3:13)

The primary motivation in Christian service must not be reward, but there is nothing wrong with looking forward to receiving rewards (2 Tim. 4:7, 8; Rev. 2:7, 10). Whatever they may be, rewards should be used to bring glory to the Savior and to extend God's kingdom. Rewards in the Lord's work always exceed our investment. For service well-rendered the Christian leader's reward is twofold in this life, according to Paul.

87

1. Gains an excellent standing. The word (*bathmos*) that is translated as "standing" means "step," a step on a staircase. The person who serves well gains for himself a good standing. It is doubtful that this suggests promotion from one position to another (from deacon to overseer). Probably what is meant is that through faithful service a ministerial leader gains a position of real influence. The one who performs his tasks well has the respect and esteem of the church and strong influence among believers.

2. Gains great assurance in his faith in Jesus Christ. The term "assurance" (*parrēsia*) contains the ideas of confidence and boldness. The reward of a good servant of God is real confidence and boldness in his own personal faith. The result of doing his work well in the church is a clear conscience, and he thus attains boldness in his faith that rests on and centers in Jesus Christ. He has greater boldness in sharing his faith with others and stronger assurance of his own salvation.

III. Conclusion

The personal standards are very high for the spiritual leader: an example as a good husband and father, personal holiness, aptitude for teaching, generous hospitality, ability to get along with other people, freedom from greed, discipline at home, spiritual maturity, and a good reputation in the outside community.

The spiritual leader should be a person of unquestionable character; but as Paul knew so well, the church is made up of ordinary people. However, that does not reduce the requirements for those responsible for the guidance and instruction of the church. No one in his own strength can meet the special requirements and fulfill the responsibilities of Christian leadership. The only way is through what Paul mentioned at the opening of his first letter to Timothy: "Grace, mercy and peace" (1:2). That is the basis of Christian character and leadership—divine grace, mercy, and peace. Therefore, a constant need is for the spiritual leader to experience the powerful reality of renewing grace, and the comforting strength of mercy, both of which issue in peace and tranquillity.

Great are the responsibilities and high are the qualifications for spiritual leadership. God, however, is good to those whom He has called to lead His people. He gives Christian leaders what is needed to do His work. He gives them guidance and direction. He gives them strength to face their responsibilities and to resist Satan's temptations. He gives them, through their own personal study and through the Holy Spirit, an understanding of the Word of Truth. He gives them grace that is sufficient to make them content and keep them from loving mammon. He gives them the gifts of the Holy Spirit, gifts to be stirred up and used (1 Tim. 4:14).

Divine grace, mercy, and peace, with all that these great concepts imply, were what shaped Paul's character and gave impetus to his service to the church. No doubt he felt insufficient in himself to maintain the high standards of Christian leadership, but he found God to be his sufficiency. Today no less should be required of those entrusted with leadership in the church. Living and serving, according to the model of 1 Timothy 3, give the spiritual leader, as they did Paul, the assurance of heaven and the exultation of heart.

> I have fought a good fight, I have finished the race, I have kept the faith. Now there is in store for me the crown of righteousness, which the Lord, the righteous Judge, will award to me on that day—and not only to me, but also to all who have longed for his appearing. [2 Tim. 4:7–8]

6

The Character of the Church

(3:14–16; 4)

The Pauline letters give evidence of a high doctrine of the church and its character. To be true to its nature a church must be a convincing witness to the truth revealed in Jesus Christ. This is to say that an outstanding and essential characteristic of a church is faithfulness to the gospel. Over and over Paul counseled Timothy to be a faithful servant. "What you heard from me, keep as the pattern of sound teaching, with faith and love in Christ Jesus. Guard the good deposit that was entrusted to you—guard it with the help of the Holy Spirit who lives in us" (2 Tim. 1:13–14). "Preach the Word; be prepared in season and out of season; correct, rebuke and encourage—with great patience and careful instruction. . . . Endure hardship, do the work of an evangelist, discharge all the duties of your ministry" (4:2–5).

Any local congregation violates its character if it departs from the gospel of Jesus Christ, but a true church believes, guards, lives by, and proclaims the gospel. The well-being of the local congregation at Ephesus prompted Paul to write Timothy. So his interest went beyond the mere organization and leadership of the church. As we have seen and will see again and again in this study, he was also devoted to maintaining and enhancing its spiritual life.

Many local churches and denominations are spiritually ill and need the healing power of the gospel. Only the church in sound health maintains the gospel and has an effective witness to the world.

I. Faith and Life of the Church (3:14–16)

The apostle had plans to visit the Ephesian congregation soon. Realizing that he might be delayed, he offered Timothy instructions about how people were to conduct themselves and perform their duties in the church. No doubt this had to do with Christian conduct in all of the relations common to the Christian fellowship. After all, the church at Ephesus was God's business, and for that reason its affairs were supremely important. In order to specify the nature of the local congregation Paul gave three designations.

A. The Church Has Three Characteristics (3:14–15)

1. "God's household." Each congregation is the house of God (*oikos*) and thus is God's dwelling place in the local fellowship of believers. As well as dwelling in each believer, God dwells corporately in the church, particularly through the Holy Spirit. He dwells in the fellowship, the society. The church as a corporate fellowship is God's sanctuary and is comprised of individuals, each of whom has become a single dwelling of God.

2. A spiritual assembly of the living God. Reference to the living God makes clear that the local church is not merely a material building but a worshiping people. This is the very heart of each local Christian fellowship, which, of course, is part of a much larger fellowship. The living God is present and at work in the world and has called into existence a people to worship and serve Him.

3. The pillar and bulwark of the truth. The gospel is the foundation on which the church is built. But here the church is described as the pillar (*stulos*, "column") and bulwark (*hedraiōma*, "buttress").[1] A congregation performs the function of a column and a buttress. It supports the truth revealed in Christ against attack and holds up the truth to the world. The solid basis of a church is the truth, but the church must be a strong defender of truth, protecting it from all danger and maintaining its integrity.

B. The Church's Faith (3:16)

Profound are the truths that are central to the Christian message. As Paul thought of these tremendous issues he declared, "The mystery of godliness is great." The term "godliness" (*eusebeia*) can be rendered as "religion" or "piety" and includes both the thought of doctrine and the practice of the Christian life. "It has its motive and purpose in a 'mystery'—i.e. in the Divine plan which is revealed in the Christian message."[2] What God did in Christ disclosed a spiritual mystery or secret. That revealed secret produces godly living.

1 Timothy 3:16 apparently is part of an ancient hymn. Early Christians used the hymn in worship and, in the present context, it provides an exposition of "the mystery of godliness." It pictures the incarnate and glorified Christ as the center of true life in earth and heaven and celebrates God's mighty saving acts in Him. Three couplets of the hymn are preserved here.

First couplet:
Incarnation at birth—"appeared in a body." God in the person of His Son veiled Himself in a human form in order to unveil Himself. This profound Christian truth has been revealed, but we still find it incomprehensible. God took to Himself lowly human nature. The life of Christ on the earth was the life of a real man as God lived in the flesh.

Vindication at resurrection—"vindicated by the Spirit." Throughout Christ's earthly life, He was rejected and despised

---

1. The New International Version translates *hedraiōma* as "foundation." It cannot be denied that that is a viable translation, but the context here seems to support "bulwark" or "buttress" in the sense of a support that secures and keeps something in place. According to 1 Corinthians 3:11, Christ alone is the foundation.

2. E. F. Scott, *The Pastoral Epistles*, (The Moffatt New Testament Commentary), p. 40.

by many, but His claims were validated by the Holy Spirit. When he was baptized in the Jordan River, the heavens were opened and the Spirit of God descended as a dove and lighted on him (Matt. 3:16; Mark 1:10). As a result of his anointing with the Spirit, demons were subject to Him; and He performed miracles (Matt. 12:22–28). At His resurrection our Lord was proven by the Holy Spirit to be the very Son of God (Rom. 1:4). He came to the earth and was put to death as a false messiah, but the Holy Spirit raised Him from the dead (Rom. 8:11) and declared Him to be in fact the Son of God, the righteous One. Through the power of the Spirit He triumphed and was vindicated as Lord.

Second couplet:

Triumph over angelic powers—"*seen by angels.*" The angelic host of heaven was witness to the drama of redemption as it unfolded before the eyes of men. Angels announced the birth of the Savior (Luke 2:9–12) and are mentioned in the accounts of His baptism, temptation, and transfiguration. Angels were witnesses to the ministry of Christ and looked upon the tremendous conflict between Christ and the power of evil.

More likely the words "seen by angels" set forth Christ's triumph over the spirit world.[3] His victory over evil spirits is found in a passage such as Colossians 2:15, "And having disarmed the powers and authorities, he made a public spectacle of them, triumphing over them by the cross." The demonic angels and principalities that control the events in this fallen age have been defeated in the cross. The crucified and risen Lord defeated the "ruler of this world" and his demonic allies who conspired to bring Him to death (John 12:31; 1 Cor. 2:8). The crucifixion was their defeat and is our assurance that we are no longer to serve them.

Proclamation to mankind—"*preached among the nations.*" The One who had triumphed over death and spiritual powers was heralded among the nations. No one had done more of this than the apostle Paul. He had proclaimed as Savior of the world

---

3. The phrase "seen by angels" is difficult, but in keeping with the motif of triumph in the hymn it is best understood to refer to the victory of Christ over spiritual forces (1 Cor. 2:8; Phil. 2:9–10; Col. 1:20).

the One who was despised and crucified but is now the triumphant Lord. The glad tidings of redemption are for all people.

Third couplet:

Acceptance throughout the world—"believed on in the world."

A great mission was initiated after the death and resurrection of Christ. At first the gospel was preached in Palestine, but the Book of Acts bears witness to its proclamation far and wide. So in just a few years Christ had been received by many people as their Savior, and the church had made a tremendous impact on society.

Acceptance in heaven—"taken up in glory." Christ came into this world, but He did not continue in it after He had completed His mission. He returned to heaven, marking a fitting climax to His triumph (Acts 1:2, 11, 22). On the earth He had been lifted up on the cross but had triumphed in resurrection. At the ascension the heavens received the victorious King. He has been lifted up to the highest degree of glory and is the exalted Lord and Head of the church.

II. Threats to the Church (4:1-5)

The apostle cited a part of an early Christian hymn that affirms the revelation of God's truth in Jesus Christ and the eternal supremacy of the risen, exalted Christ. However, he also was fully aware that error had raised its head at Ephesus and that there was opposition to the truth of the gospel.

A. The Approach of Apostasy (4:1-3a)

The rise of apostasy was an unmistakable fact. The rejection of sound doctrine was not a passing situation. Timothy and the church at Ephesus needed to understand that insidious opposition to the truth was a permanent characteristic of this age. Consider some of the details.

1. Announced by the Spirit. A number of prophecies in the Scriptures deal with false teachers and apostasy (Dan. 7:25; Matt. 24:4-12; Mark 13:22). Likely Paul was acquainted with these, but the implication is that the Spirit had distinctly made known to Paul the dangers of the rise of false teachers in the not-too-distant future. He himself warned the Christians at Thessalonica and the elders of the church at Ephesus of the rise of false teachers and the perils of heresy (2 Thess. 2:1–12; Acts 20:29–30). The Holy Spirit made clear to Paul that in the latter times error would flourish. The latter times are "the last days" of 2 Timothy 3:1, Mark 13, and Acts 2:17. This is the period initiated by the coming of Jesus Christ and into which the church entered at Pentecost. It is the time between the times— the time between the first and the second coming of Christ.

At the first advent of our Lord the old age had begun to pass away and the last days had dawned. This being true, Timothy was living in the last days, and so are we. What the Holy Spirit had predicted of the future related to Timothy's own ministry. Men were already distorting the truth of the gospel. Timothy was in the midst of the storm, and he was not to be overly optimistic, hoping that it would soon pass. Paul offered him no such hope. We, too, need to be clear about the troubles and perils that will befall us if we stand firm for the gospel.

2. Identifiable by signs. The falling away from sound teaching is specified in a twofold manner. The first sign was the activity of deceiving spirits and doctrines taught by demons. Deceiving spirits were demons. Their design was to frustrate God's purpose and to lead astray God's people. To serve their cause, they did not hesitate to disseminate falsehoods and to distort the faith that Christ entrusted to the church for safekeeping. Like Paul, we must understand our opposition. "For our struggle is not against flesh and blood, but against the rulers, against the authorities, against the powers of this dark world and against the spiritual forces of evil in the heavenly realms" (Eph. 6:12).

The second sign was that some people had become agents of demons and had forsaken the truth and had become hypocritical liars. These men were advocating deceitful doctrines inspired by demons. They made themselves appear different than they were. They had abandoned the truth and purity of the gospel. They saw nothing wrong with lying. As Paul observed, their "consciences have been seared [*kautēriazō*, "cauterized"] as with a hot iron." The conscience in that condition is callous. Sensitivity to the truth is lost, and lying can become habitual.

3. Teachings issuing from demons. Here Paul mentioned two. The first was the rejection of the institution of marriage.[4] This assumes that to please God one must become an ascetic. Of course, the idea is that the body and everything connected with it is evil. On the basis of this assumption logic would lead to the conclusion that marriage is evil. But, on the contrary, the married state is normal and has divine sanction. In fact, marriage was instituted by God. The value and dignity of this divine institution must be defended against those who denounce it by extolling celibacy.

The second error is insistence on abstinence from certain foods. This was an outgrowth of the assumption that all matter is evil. Food is matter and thus evil. Such a view conflicts with God's verdict that all things He created were good (Gen. 1:31). Asceticism does not result in genuine spirituality. Though fasting has its place, its value can be overemphasized.

B. Right Use of Creation (4:3b-5)

What the false teachers advocated went beyond the implications of the gospel. To counter the errors of these people, Paul set forth a number of truths.

1. "Everything God created is good." Nothing came from the creative hand of God that works to the detriment of mankind. All is designed for their welfare, enjoyment, and happiness. The curse of sin disrupted the created order, but creation still is

---

4. William L. Lane, "1 Tim. IV. 1-3. An Early Instance of Over-Realized Eschatology?," *New Testament Studies* 11 (January 1965): 164-169, explains the doctrine of the false teachers to be due to their failure to distinguish their present refreshing, which the resurrection of Christ initiated, from the consummation to be realized in the yet future resurrection. 2 Timothy 2:17-18 states that Hymenaeus and Philetus taught that the resurrection was already past. The obvious conclusion would be that the Christian community had entered fully into the age to come and the resurrection lay in the past. Therefore Jesus' teaching that in the resurrection men neither marry nor give their children in marriage demanded that marriage cease. It is possible that this was the thinking of the false teachers mentioned in 1 Timothy 4:1-3.

fundamentally good. It serves the well-being of all in many ways, especially as long as men use it as God intended.

2. Everything God created is to be received with thanksgiving. Abundant are God's gifts in creation. Unless they are received with gratitude, they are not seen as gifts of God. Many people enjoy the blessings and benefits of creation, but they fail to receive with thanksgiving what God has created. Food, a gift of God, is to be received with thanksgiving. Gratitude for the gifts of God does not lead us to asceticism but to reception of those gifts with proper appreciation and thanksgiving. The Christian has special reason for acknowledging with gratitude that all material things are from above.

3. Everything is consecrated by the reading of Scripture and the prayer of thanksgiving. Eating and drinking are daily activities, but for the children of God these should be more than satisfying one's appetite. If before a meal the Word of God is read and prayer is offered, partaking of food and drink is a spiritual act as well as a way of satisfying the appetite. The meal is consecrated (*haiazetai,* "is caused to be set apart, is sanctified"). It is removed from profane or common use. Having been consecrated by Word and prayer, it is set aside for holy use.

III. Ways to Preserve the Integrity of the Church (4:6-10)

Important to the integrity of the Christian congregation at Ephesus was Timothy's faithful discharge of his ministry. God had called him and equipped him for the work, but mere denunciation of those who were in error would not improve the situation. The most effective means of dealing with them and maintaining the integrity of the church's message was by Timothy's being "a good minister of Christ Jesus." Paul identified what is fitting for that kind of minister (*diakonos,* "servant").

A. Proclaim the Truth (4:6)

Like that of any minister, Timothy's preaching and teaching should have both a positive and a negative side. The truth must be made clear, and errors must be pointed out. That is probably what Paul had in mind when he wrote, ". . . you point these things out to the brothers." This does not mean to issue orders. The word translated as "point" (*hupotithēmi*) means "to lay before, to counsel, to suggest." A good minister must call to the believers' remembrance the truths of Scripture, but he must not be harsh and dogmatic in teaching the truth and in pointing out error. Love must always temper the minister's denouncement of error.

B. Reject Speculation (4:7a)

Timothy was instructed to "have nothing to do with godless myths and old wives' tales." These were false teachings in contrast to sound doctrine. The word "godless" (*bebēlos*) literally refers to that which is worthy of being trodden under foot and thus is utterly profane and spiritually bankrupt. The addition of the words "old wives'" reinforces the idea. Therefore, what the false teachers advocated were worthless fancies. Their doctrines were "myths" and "tales" (*muthoi*) that old women told to children. They had no spiritual value.

Timothy was advised to shun such superstitious trivialities. A servant of God can get sidetracked from God's eternal truths and get caught up in insignificant issues. To prevent this he must engage himself in the study of God's Word and in sound teaching.

C. Train Himself in Godliness (4:7b-10)

Paul admonished Timothy to keep on training himself in godly living. The athlete spared no effort to develop his body in gymnastic exercises. So the apostle's young friend was to be equally devoted to training himself to be a good servant of Jesus Christ. It was not to be a self-centered, ascetic exercise to attain religious perfection. His vigorous spiritual development was to serve the glory of God. A number of truths stand out in Paul's instructions.

1. Spiritual training "has value for all things." Spiritual training holds "promise for both the present life and the life to come."

But in contrast, physical training only profits a little; it improves the athlete's body and gives him additional stamina. Physical strength and vigor are good, but the benefits are of short duration. Vigorous training in godly living, however, brings both present and eternal dividends. The rewards of godly living are reaped in this life and the life to come. So godliness is valuable for all things—profitable in every way, producing rewards for the present and future. "Irrespective of his present earthly circumstances, a Christian may fairly be said to have the best of both worlds."[5]

2. Spiritual training demands real effort. The words of Paul here are to the point: "we labor and strive." Both of the words, "labor" (*kopiaō*, "to work hard") and "strive" (*agōnizomai*, "struggle"), speak of the tremendous efforts and dedication called for in the work of the gospel. An excellent servant of God expends his energy to the point of exhaustion if necessary. He must not come to expect an easy time but must put forth his best efforts in the struggle against the powers of darkness. Such a struggle is absolutely necessary if he is to succeed in bringing people out of darkness into the marvelous light of the gospel.

3. The value of spiritual training is secure. As he undergoes arduous training, the servant of the Lord must fix his "hope in the living God." The simple reason is that God as the living God alone can bestow life now and hereafter. Hope in the living God means that now and in the age to come the believer's eternal life will be solidly founded and secure. Assured hope warrants the endurance of strenuous training and perseverance in the faith by the believer.

IV. Ways to Arm Christians Against False Teaching (4:11-16)

Paul had urged the importance of self-discipline. He continued with that emphasis, but the need for self-discipline is

---

5. Donald Guthrie, *The Pastoral Epistles,* (Tyndale New Testament Commentaries), p. 95.

related here more directly to Timothy's character as a church leader. The young man could be a real source of power and influence against unsound doctrine among the believers.

A. Commanding and Teaching (4:11)

The phrase "command and teach" is an unusual combination of terms, but it is fitting. The word "command" (*paraggellō*) means "to transmit a message or to command someone." The idea is that Timothy was to constantly charge the Christians to have nothing to do with "godless myths and old wives' tales" and to urge them not to reject as evil what God created for man's benefit. Likewise he was to be constantly faithful in teaching the believers sound doctrine, informing them that godly living was profitable in every way.

B. Being an Example to the Faithful (4:12)

Because of his youth Timothy was at some disadvantage. It had been about fifteen years since he had become Paul's associate. No doubt he was older than what Paul's language might suggest to us. In the ancient world a person between thirty and forty years old was considered young.[6] Timothy was still a young man, especially to be the leader of the elders in the church at Ephesus. The concern was that Timothy be a model Christian leader so that neither the young nor old would despise his youth. Paul admonished Timothy to excel in five personal qualities. The church and its leaders would do well to heed this admonition.

1. An example in speech. Whether in public or in private, Timothy's speech should be exemplary. If so, nothing would be said that would crush others or bring reproach upon his ministry.

2. An example in life. Timothy's lifestyle and his relationships with others would not be offensive, but rather his conduct would affirm that he was a man of God.

---

6. The word for "young" (*neotēs*) could describe a person up to forty years old. Some scholars have suggested that at the time Timothy was between the ages of thirty-four and thirty-nine.

3. An example in love. Genuine love manifests itself in a real concern for the welfare of those within and without the church. Love was to temper Timothy's relationships with others, even his dealings with those in error. A concern for the welfare of all is an excellent way of sharing Christ's love with others.

4. An example in faith. As a servant of the Lord, Timothy should be an example of living by faith. His right relationship with God should be evidenced by his full commitment to the work of God. He must have faith to exercise the spiritual gifts granted to him for ministry.

5. An example in purity. This word "purity" (*hagneia*) includes integrity of heart as well as chastity in the matters of sex. Such purity issues from conformity to God's will in thought and deed. There would have been no real reason for criticizing Timothy because of his youthfulness if he was an example in speech, life, love, faith, and purity.

C. Diligence in Liturgical Functions (4:13)

At this time Paul had made plans to visit Ephesus again. In the meantime he desired that Timothy be faithful in the discharge of his ministerial responsibilities, particularly the public reading of Scripture and preaching and teaching the truth. Here is a threefold ministry.

1. Reading of Scripture. Public reading of the Word is an essential dimension of worship. The Bible is God's Word, and God speaks through it. If the Scriptures are really valued as the Word of God, a prominent place will be given to them in the worship of the congregation. The wise choice of passages and the effective reading of them will enhance both the worship and the relevance of Scripture to the community of believers.

2. Preaching (paraklēsis, *"exhortation, encouragement"*). The minister is commissioned by God to speak the divine Word. God speaks through preaching. The truth that was once for all delivered to the saints needs to be interpreted and proclaimed. It was a practice of Jesus to expound the Scriptures. In Luke 4:16–30 He interpreted the Scripture that He had read in the synagogue. An exposition normally followed the reading of the Scripture in the synagogue worship. In Acts 13:15 Paul and his associates were invited by the rulers of the synagogue to give a message of exhortation after the reading from the law and the prophets.

Since those early days, preaching has had a vital place in the Christian church. Solid exposition of the Word joined with exhortation and encouragement will show people the relevance of Jesus Christ and provide a firm basis and impetus for Christian living.

3. Teaching (didaskalia, *"doctrine"*). The servant of the Lord not only is to preach the Word but also is to teach it. It is common to make a distinction between "proclamation" (*kerugma*) and "teaching" (*didachē*), the former being a proclamation of the saving work of Christ to unbelievers with an invitation to repent and the latter being instruction in Christian ethics and living.[7] However, care should be taken not to press this distinction too far. The difference may be more in style than in content.

But needless to say, instruction in doctrine and moral precepts of Scripture are important. The Bible needs to be explained so that people can have a sound faith and establish their lives upon eternal truth.

There should be a balance in public worship. Some neglect the reading of Scriptures; others are unconcerned about preaching; still others never teach. Real worship of God includes all three.

D. Constantly Using His Gift (4:14)

A special endowment of the Spirit had been bestowed on Timothy for ministry. Like any spiritual gift, it was a gift of grace (*charisma*), a gift that finds its roots in God's grace (*charis*). The gift is not identified by name, but it was probably

---

7. The classic work on the subject is *The Apostolic Preaching and Its Developments* by C. H. Dodd.

the ability to discern between truth and error while teaching believers the doctrine of Christ.

Prophecy had accompanied the bestowal of the gift. Apparently an inspired prophet revealed the nature of Timothy's call (1:18). By the Holy Spirit he was equipped for a special ministry. In fact, the spiritual gift was conferred upon the young man when the elders laid their hands on him. On that occasion Paul must have been present (2 Tim. 1:6).

The young man would do well to remember that he had been set aside for a specific work and had been equipped by the Holy Spirit. He was not to neglect his gift. God had granted it, but he was responsible for using it. Spiritual gifts must never be left unused. They are essential to the work and the mission of the church.

E. Meditating on These Things (4:15–16)

Constant attention given to sound doctrine and to the matters of ministry would cultivate the faith of the believers and preserve the integrity of the church in the face of error. Paul instructed Timothy to "give yourself wholly to them." His heart and mind were to be wrapped up in the work of the ministry. This would have very definite consequences.

1. Timothy's spiritual progress would be clear to everyone. People inside and outside of the church would take note of his growth in the Lord. No doubt that kind of Christian development would affect his pulpit ministry. What would impress those to whom he preached would not be a lesser thing, such as profound orations or attractiveness of personality, but his godly character and sound teaching.

Depth in God and in His Word is needed in pulpits today. Intellectual laziness is an abomination to God. The minister is tempted to devote himself to peripheral matters related to ministry rather than to the study and the exposition of Scripture. But the minister who has a rich spiritual life and is a devoted student of the Scriptures will be looked upon as a real man of God.

2. *Purity of life and soundness in doctrine will serve a double purpose.* These characteristics would help Timothy to work out his own salvation as well as help others to do the same. That is, he would save himself and those who heard him. Salvation is by grace, but a minister's godly life and sound teaching are factors in bringing people to salvation. A careless and unfaithful minister can play havoc with the faith of God's people, whereas a man of God who is devoted to keeping his own life straight and his doctrine sound will bring the message of eternal salvation to many.

V. Conclusion

At Ephesus there existed a community of faith that was described by Paul as "God's household, ... the church of the living God, the pillar and foundation of the truth." As is the case with all true Christian communities, the Ephesian church was sustained by the gospel. Loyalty to its content included the reality of the incarnation, the triumph of the risen Christ, the exaltation of the Savior "above all heavens," and confidence in the power of the gospel to minister to basic human problems and to call men and women to be reconciled to God.

The Christian community in Ephesus faced difficult times. There were satanic influences in that church. Men took positions that were at variance with the clear teaching of Scripture and promoted living and thinking that represented a decisive departure from Christian truth.

Paul urged Timothy to stand firm against doctrines inspired by demons and to be diligent in the exercise of his ministry on behalf of the church. He was to give careful attention to his own life so he would be a personal example of what he taught and preached. His preaching was to be something more than a personal testimony of what God had done for him. The content of his sermons was not to be his own religious experience but the Scriptures. His preaching was to be a Word from God, a Word about what God had done in Christ for all who believe.

The need for the proclamation and the defense of the gospel is as urgent now as it was then. This need can be met only by men and women, equipped by the Holy Spirit for service, who are personally committed to sound doctrine and the Christian life. By no other means can we ensure the preservation of the integrity of the church and its message.

Proper Relationships

(5:1–2, 17–25; 6:1–2)

The church is a community of believers. God has called together in the church people from different walks of life. Normally a church is composed of people who differ in educational background, in psychological make-up, in social standing, in age, and in spiritual maturity. The essential basis of their fellowship is not due to their attraction to each other, but rather their fellowship, grounded in God who called them together.

The church embraces all people with their individual differences and must learn to deal with frictions and disagreements. All confusion and conflict that beset the church are not over the great issues of Christian doctrine or due to the social, racial, and economic differences of its members. At times the source of dissension in the body of Christ has been the church's leaders. Some of them have not learned to act with meekness and speak in love. Inevitably the result has been unnecessary alienation and confusion in the church.

The apostle Paul understood the importance of proper relationships in the church. He did not fail to caution Timothy about how he should relate to the various groups that made up the Christian community of Ephesus.

I. Conduct Toward the Young and the Old of Both Sexes (5:1–2)

As is true for all servants of God, Timothy's interactions with others were occasions for ministry. The quality of his relationships was at the heart of his faith. His relationship with God was to provide the framework and determine how he related to others. He was to remember that the church is the family of God and treat its members as fathers, mothers, brothers, and sisters. The old and young were to be treated with respect and discretion.

A. Older People (5:1a, 2a)

1. Admonish an older man as a father. The older man in the church was to be treated as Timothy would treat his own father. A man of advanced age was not to be rebuked severely or dealt with harshly. If it became necessary to discipline an older man because of his sins, that was to be done with tact and moderation. The word translated here as "exhort" (*parakaleō*) is rich in meaning and includes ideas such as "to appeal to, urge, exhort, encourage." Hard words would crush, but plain words properly spoken and discipline fairly administered would be corrective.

2. Treat the older women as mothers. Timothy was to show respect for the older women in the congregation. If an older woman needed correction, he must deal directly with her. He must not lose patience with her but should maintain respect for her as he would for his own mother. Patience and respect are conducive to cooperation. Advice offered with love and tact is likely to be heeded.

B. Young People (5:1b, 2b)

A wise minister knows how to conduct himself with the young as well as with the old.

1. Younger men. Timothy himself was a young man and was instructed to treat the younger men as brothers. If he did that, he would consider them to be his peers. His fellowship with them would be characterized by tolerance, equality, sharing, and reciprocity.

To be sure, as a man of God, Timothy had authority. When it was necessary he was not to hesitate to exercise it. But he was to put forth every effort to maintain good relations with those under his charge. The admonition of Romans 12:18 is applicable to all Christians. "If it is possible, . . . live at peace with everyone."

2. *Younger women.* As a spiritual counselor, Timothy was placed in a delicate position. His relationships with the younger women were to be characterized by purity. He was to treat them as he would expect his own sister to be treated. It was absolutely imperative that his affection for them remain within the bounds of perfect propriety. Every minister's moral integrity is essential to the integrity of his ministry.

There is to be true fraternity between the pastor and his flock. However, all relationships within the household of faith must be in accordance with dignity and propriety.

II. Life in the Community of Faith (5:17-25)

Here Paul touched on three of the most vexing problems of today: the ethics of rewards, the ethics of discipline, and the ethics of personal integrity. They were delicate concerns for Timothy, too, and were crucial to personal relationships in the church. Mindful of this, Paul gave to his young friend instructions on these sensitive issues.

A. The Ethics of Reward (5:17-18)

Paul has spoken of the elder in 1 Timothy 5:1. That seems to have been a general way of referring to the older Christian men. Chapter 3 of the Epistle, where the qualifications of the elders are described, has the church leaders in view. Again in 5:17-18 attention is drawn to the elders as church leaders and more specifically to the church's reluctance to compensate the elders.

1. *Double honor.* The elders were spiritual leaders in the household of God. Those who discharged their responsibilities well were due double honor. According to verse 18, financial support is meant. Therefore, the term *double honor* must refer to "ample remuneration."[1] No doubt Paul was aware that a

---

1. A number of interpretations have been offered. One is that the phrase means

congregation could forget its obligations to its leaders and take their work for granted. Those who direct the affairs of the church well deserve a good salary.

Among the elders were those who apparently devoted themselves to administration and the oversight of the spiritual life of the congregation. The others no doubt did likewise; but they also engaged constantly in preaching and teaching. Already in local congregations were those who devoted themselves to preaching the word and expounding doctrinal truths.[2] They were called to the ministry of proclamation and had shown special aptitude and spiritual endowments for preaching and teaching. These elders were especially worthy of double honor.

2. Scriptural teaching. The apostles appealed to passages from sacred Scripture to support the teaching that the laborers in word and doctrine are worthy to receive adequate pay.

a. "'Do not muzzle the ox while it is treading out the grain'" *(Deut. 25:4).* The verse enjoined on the Jews the practice of not muzzling the ox as it was driven over the grain lying on the threshing floor. The hoofs of the ox shook the grain loose from the stalk. At the same time the ox was to be free to eat of the grain. This custom taught that consideration was to be shown to the beast of burden.

Such consideration was to be shown to every worker, including those who labored in word and doctrine. God sanctions the principle that those who devote most of their time to the service of the church are to receive adequate remuneration. As workers in God's vineyard, ministers (clergy) have the right to partake of the fruits of their works.

---

twice as much pay as the widows or the deacons received. There is no indication that the widows or the deacons were paid. Another explanation is that the elder is to receive double honor in the sense of twice as much respect. No doubt honor in the sense of respect may be implied, but remuneration seems to be what Paul has in view in verse 17. The word *honor* (*timē*) is used in Acts 4:34; 7:16; 1 Corinthians 6:20 in the sense of price or pay. In light of what is said in verse 18 financial support must be understood as the primary meaning.

2. All the elders were expected to assume a measure of the responsibility in teaching (1 Tim. 3:2; Titus 1:8, 9), but there were those who had gifts for this kind of ministry. They were the specialists and gave much of their time to preaching and teaching.

b. "The worker deserves his wages" (Luke 10:7).[3] The apostle apparently had these same words in mind when he wrote, "the Lord has commanded that those who preach the gospel should receive their living from the gospel" (1 Cor. 9:14). According to the Old Testament and the teaching of Jesus, the laborers in word and doctrine deserve to be maintained at the expense of the church.

As we have already seen, Scripture deplores money-grabbing, especially when the guilty are those who labor for Christ (1 Tim. 3:3). But it equally deplores a miserly attitude where a church begrudges and in some instances denies a faithful servant of the gospel an adequate salary. Work in the gospel should never be done merely for material reward, but a congregation that has the financial resources should not fail to discharge its obligation to a faithful worker in God's vineyard.

B. The Ethics of Discipline (5:19–21)

As leaders of a congregation the elders were naturally subject to criticism. They would need protection from malicious and unfounded charges. At this point Paul shifted his attention from rewarding elders to disciplining them.

1. Dealing with offenders.

a. Be fair. A charge (*katēgoria,* "legal accusation") was to be entertained against no one unless it was "brought by two or three witnesses." This reaffirmed Deuteronomy 19:15, which asserts that at the mouth of two or three witnesses a matter would be established. A church leader was not to be brought to trial without at least two or three witnesses. The evidence has to be sufficient before action can be initiated against a servant of God. Credence must not be given to charges without convincing evidence. Satan attacks the servants of God by slander and gossip, but they must not be condemned by rumor or by one

---

3. How could Paul quote from the Gospel according to Luke? Paul and Luke were friends. According to Colossians 4:14 and Philemon 24, Luke was with Paul during the apostle's first Roman imprisonment. Therefore, Paul is likely quoting either from the Gospel of Luke or from a collection of sayings that Luke used in writing his Gospel.

witness. They deserve fair treatment and protection of their character from malicious hearsay.

b. Be firm. Once a church leader was found to be sinning, discipline was to be clear-cut and decisive. As Paul instructed, "Those who sin[4] are to be rebuked publicly, so that the others may take warning." Discipline was to be administered in public so that the other leaders and the church members would have been warned against doing wrong. Those leaders who had proved to be unworthy of their trust were to be exposed and rebuked publicly. Correcting wayward leaders in the presence of others would put godly fear in the heart of those tempted to sin and would serve as an admonition to all the believers.

The church must not take sin lightly. It must be dealt with forthrightly. The sin of wayward leaders cannot be overlooked. When discipline is administered in public, the church will profit and outsiders will respect the church for such action.

2. Judging conduct without personal bias. Evil men have been shielded; innocent men have been condemned. To avoid this Paul charged Timothy to administer discipline without partiality or favoritism. This was a solemn charge before God, Christ Jesus, and the elect angels. The reference here to the three witnesses stressed the importance of maintaining discipline in the church. It was no light matter. The instructions to Timothy were issued under God's approval. God through Christ will judge all men. The elect angels are also associated with the final judgment (2 Thess. 1:7; Heb. 12:22; Rev. 14:15, 17–20). These angels did not fall; they kept their exalted state (Jude 6).

Timothy would do well to exercise caution and impartiality in his appraisal of the conduct of others. On the day of judgment he would have to account to God for his handling of discipline in the church. Jesus had solemnly warned that he would disown unworthy servants "when he comes in his glory and in the glory of the Father and of the holy angels" (Luke 9:26).

Discipline must be fair and impartial. Judgment is not to be

---

4. The present participle *sinning* (*hamartanontos*) can be understood to refer to habitual sinners, but it is difficult to see that such people would have been among the elders of the church.

formed on the basis of personal like or dislike. All the facts must be examined without a leaning to this side or that side. Guilt must not be determined on the basis of personal bias but with caution and impartiality. The church has to deal with wrong-doing, but it should not withhold its ministry from the guilty.

C. The Ethics of Personal Integrity (5:22–25)

Personal integrity has much to do with relationships in a local community of Christians. Fellowship of believers rests on the confidence they have in one another. Integrity goes far in building solid relationships and effective ministries in the church. The seriousness with which Timothy appointed people to serve as church leaders underscores this fact. Paul gave his friend some guidelines for selecting leaders.

1. Give only pure people appointments in the church. The admonition of Paul here is: "Do not be hasty in the laying on of hands."[5] This refers to the setting aside for specific service (2 Tim. 1:6).[6] Untried men are not to be appointed as leaders in the household of faith. A person's qualifications are of utmost importance. A careful examination of the candidate is in order. That kind of caution increases significantly the possibility of appointing only the worthy and the qualified. The consequences can be serious when a person is appointed hastily. Disciplinary problems may arise. The removal of an unqualified or irrespon-sible church leader is usually painful. The exercise of restraint in making appointments is wise.

2. Keep yourself pure. If Timothy appointed bad men to important church work, he would share the responsibility for their sins. Their sin would bring reproach on the Savior and on

---

5. This directive must have been intended for the elders as well as for Timothy (1 Tim. 4:14).

6. There is another interpretation—the restoration of deposed elders. It might have been a practice to lay hands on a backslider who returned to the church in a repentant spirit. Some scholars have followed this interpretation because they are convinced that it is in keeping with the immediate context in which reference is made to publicly rebuking the wayward elder. According to this view, Timothy was not to be hasty in restoring him.

the good name of the church. Timothy would be held accountable for their mischief and blamed for the damage they did to the church. By appointing unworthy men to responsible church positions he was guilty of participating (*koinōneō*) in their sins.[7]

In the interest of his own credibility Timothy must be careful to set aside only people of noble character for special service. The personal charge—"Keep yourself pure"—called for Timothy to be upright in all things. He was to take every precaution to appoint only good individuals to work with him. In fact, they were to be upright and pure in all matters.

a. Purity is not asceticism.[8] The false teachers advocated ascetic practices, denying that everything God made was good (1 Tim. 4:4–5) and forgetting that for the pure all things are pure (Titus 1:15). Purity is important, but it does not require ascetic abstinence, as the false teachers apparently were advocating. Their understanding of purity was too rigid, making it synonymous with asceticism. For them the human body was evil rather than good and must be treated as such. Timothy, following the dictates of strict asceticism, apparently had refused to use wine as medicine. He was advised by Paul to stop drinking only water and to take a little wine for his health's sake. The water could have been dangerous and could have caused indigestion or dysentery.

b. Wine has medicinal value. In the ancient world wine was a common medication. It was recommended to Timothy as medicine, not as a beverage. He was to drink a little wine for his physical condition. E. F. Scott's observation is to the point:

> It has to be noted that the verse is meant, not to advocate the use of wine, but to protest against a type of doctrine which would rule out the whole physical side of man's life as evil. Taken in this sense it helps to illustrate the admirable sanity which is everywhere characteristic of this writer. He recognizes that the body has its rights, and is impatient with saints who will not behave like normal human beings.[9]

---

7. The construction of the negative (*mēde*) with the imperative (*koinōnei*) urges Timothy to stop what he was already guilty of doing.

8. Verse 23 seems to be a brief parenthetical statement.

9. *The Pastoral Epistles,* (The Moffatt New Testament Commentary), p. 69.

3. Discern good and evil. At times good and evil are hard to distinguish. Because of this it is not always easy to determine the true character of a person. This must have been a problem that Timothy faced in the examination of prospective leaders for the church. Even so, good and evil are radically different and the true nature of a man's deeds will eventually come to light.

a. Conspicuous and concealed sins. The sins of some are quite obvious and plain to all. Their bad reputations go before them to "the place of judgment." They are condemned by their own deeds before they are judged. The type of judgment is not specified here, but it probably is the judgment of God. The sins of those who are openly evildoers will ultimately bring them into the judgment of God. Their sins are leading them to the place of judgment.

On the other hand, there are those who are evildoers, but their sins are not quite so evident. The sins of these trail behind them and come to light later. Usually a careful examination of such people uncovers their sins. The unworthy should be disqualified from leadership functions in the church.

The significant point is that "hasty actions rely on first impressions, but these impressions are often deceptive. Unworthy men might be chosen, whose moral culpability lies deeper than the surface."[10]

b. Conspicuous and concealed good works. Most persons' good works are evident; their good works are their adornment. But there are those who choose not to be obvious. Many of these persons' fine qualities and qualifications are not so apparent and sometimes they are unknown. Such persons can easily be overlooked. Their good qualities and deeds will eventually become known. Time will reveal the bad and the good of men. Caution is imperative in selecting leaders of the church.

III. Christians in an Unchristian Society (6:1–2)

Slavery was a problem for the early church. There were both slaves and masters in the church. The Christian slaves were

---

10. Donald Guthrie, *The Pastoral Epistles*, (Tyndale New Testament Commentaries), p. 109.

equal to their Christian masters in the churches. They were treated as brothers and sisters, but the slaves did not have equal standing with their masters in ordinary life. As a result the slave-master relationship had become a pressing problem. The church would have made a fatal mistake to have encouraged the slaves to revolt. The inevitable result would have been anarchy, civil war, and mass murder. The gospel method of reformation never has been violence but rather transformation.

The only solution was the abolition of this evil institution that denied individual worth and dignity. However, slavery was a deeply rooted system and woven into the fabric of that society. Being realistic, the apostle recognized that the time was not favorable to the abolition of slavery. But he did offer Christian directives. These could have positive value for slave-master relationships until the ultimate solution to the problem.

A. Christian Slaves and Their Unsaved Masters
(6:1)

Slaves who become Christians could have thought that they should be delivered from such a hard lot. Or they might have been tempted to have a superior attitude toward their unbelieving masters. Having found liberty in Christ, slaves were to continue to serve their masters. Both the manner and reason are specified.

1. The manner. Though their masters were unbelievers, the Christian slaves were to treat them with full respect. No doubt many of the owners were unworthy. At this point, Paul did not deal with the possible severity of the unbelieving masters. Regardless of their masters' conduct, the slaves were to be Christians and serve them with proper respect.

2. The reason. By being respectful and dependable, the slaves would be effective witnesses for Christ. Otherwise they would bring their masters' ridicule and disdain on God's name and the gospel. The masters would have said that God and Christian doctrine were responsible for the misconduct of the slaves. The truth is that liberty in Christ should have made slaves better slaves—more courteous and more reliable than other slaves.

Their motivation was to be good representatives of the gospel. The lot of the Christian slaves was hard, but the servant is not above his Lord.

B. Christian Slaves and Their Believing Masters
   (6:2)

Slaves with Christian masters were fortunate. Having believing masters, they could have had two particular temptations. They could have been tempted to take advantage of the fact that they and their masters belonged to the same brotherhood. Because of this, they could have taken liberties and become lazy.

These slaves also could have been tempted to show less respect (*kataphroneō*, "to think against, to despise") for their masters. Their newfound freedom in Christ did not liberate them from the hard realities of slavery. Nevertheless they were not to look down upon Christian slave owners. They were instructed to show respect for their Christian masters. Otherwise they would have been unchristian.

Paul went on to say that Christian slaves were to serve (literally, "to slave for") the Christian masters more diligently. He indicated the manner of service and the reason for it.

1. The manner. Christian masters were to be served "even better" (*mallon*, "more"). Christian slaves who had the good fortune of having Christian masters should not have been careless about their work. To the contrary, they should serve their believing masters better than they would have served unbelieving masters.

2. The reason. The masters who benefited from the slaves' service were fellow believers and were "dear [*agapētos*, "beloved"] to them." This was all the more reason why the believing slaves should have served their masters faithfully. The master's commitment to Christ should have been a strong incentive for the Christian slave to serve well. The masters would benefit from the good service (*euergesia*, "good deeds") of their slaves. However, such service would have probably proved to be a benefit for the slaves. Likely the Christian masters would have

117

rewarded them for their good deeds of service. In that case, the slaves, too, would have been benefactors.

Nowhere in his letters did Paul endorse the institution of slavery. No doubt he was strongly opposed to it. He sought to undermine slavery, particularly by teaching that both Christian slaves and masters belonged to the same brotherhood. However, he knew that the problem could not be solved in a moment and, too, that evil practices in society were changed only as people were transformed.

The church has a message for society, and the power of the gospel must be brought to bear on the evils of society. But it takes time for the leaven of the gospel to work.

IV. Conclusion

Strong relationships are essential to the church carrying out its mission. These were the kinds of relationships that Paul sought to foster in the church. The credibility of Timothy's ministry and the effective discharge of his responsibilities rested on the quality of his relationships in the church. Convinced of this fact, Paul called on his young friend to be a model in his human relations. His instructions remind us of a number of personal qualities that should be characteristic of the relationships of a Christian leader. In fact, these qualities should be characteristic of the relationships of all Christians.

The first is kindness and propriety. The older people are to be treated with respect. If disciplining one of them becomes necessary, the servant of God is not to assume the role of a dictator. As a son would admonish his father or mother, so he is to deal with the older Christians. Discipline must never be unduly severe, but it must be administered so that respect is maintained.

The young people also are important. The man of God is to build solid relationships with them so that they will know that he is their friend and that they can look to him for counsel and encouragement. His personal relationships with them must always be in keeping with what is fitting and proper.

A second personal quality is the giving of honor to those who deserve honor. When Paul spoke of "double honor," his main concern seems to have been adequate remuneration for those who engaged in preaching and teaching. Liberality in pay is proper and a concrete expression of honor for those laboring in word and doctrine. But needless to say, many are faithfully committed to the work of the local church and serve without any financial compensation. The church does well to honor these people for their ministry. Recognition of their gifts and talents makes them aware of their value in the kingdom's work and serves to build and maintain good relationships in the church.

The third personal quality is fairness in judging conduct. When charges are made against a Christian, the evidence is to be examined carefully. No one should be made a victim of pettiness or condemned on unfounded charges. No action is to be taken when the evidence is insufficient. If wrongdoing is proved, correction must be clear-cut and forthright. Sin cannot be taken lightly or overlooked. The administration of discipline in fairness, without favoritism or prejudice, fosters confidence in the leadership of the church and does much to build relationships based on trust.

The fourth personal quality is integrity in church appointments. Estimating a person's fitness for leadership in the church is not always an easy matter. Capable people, willing to assume the responsibilities of leadership in the household of faith, have been hard to find at times. Too often appointments have been made for the wrong reasons. Some people have been given a position to maintain their interest in the church, others because of family ties, and still others because they were active campaigners and enjoyed public recognition. Caution is to be the rule in the appointment of church workers so that the unworthy are excluded. This is so important to proper relationships in the church.

The fifth personal quality is wisdom. Most congregations are made up of people of different races, different age groups, different educational levels, and different social standing. The same was the case in the first-century churches in which slaves and masters worshiped together. The gospel is still transforming all kinds of men and women of different cultures and bringing them together to worship God. Their differences are not abolished in Christ, but in the body of Christ they meet on equal terms. They are all brothers and sisters, but their differences create tension and even discord in the body of Christ. Where these situations are handled with wisdom and discretion strong and enduring relationships are built.

Building and maintaining good relationships require a conscious reliance on the ministry of the Holy Spirit. Relationships characterized by kindness, propriety, and integrity cannot be sustained by mere human effort. Honoring those who deserve honor, administering fair and firm discipline, and applying wisdom when tension and conflict develop are beyond mere human capability. No one but the Holy Spirit can implant the qualities that will bring about and maintain proper relationships. Solid relationships are rooted in the work of the Holy Spirit and believers' openness to His leading.

8

A Sense of Family in the Church

(5:3–16)

T he church is God's household and has its life through the redemptive ministry of Christ. God's home is not the tangible structure of the church. Of course we call church buildings houses of God, but where God makes His home is in the sort of fellowship found in a family. God has entered into intimate communion with each believer and has made His home in the fellowship of His people. On the earth He dwells in the hearts and the fellowship of the redeemed.

Paul was convinced of this truth. He reminded the Ephesian believers of this when he wrote, "And in him [Christ] you too are being built together to become a dwelling in which God lives by his Spirit" (Eph. 2:22). A congregation of believers is a local manifestation of the household of God. By God's grace they have been brought into a deep, intimate relationship with each other. Under the heavenly Father they are inescapably a family and are to share the burdens and the blessings of one another.

As a family, the church has a responsibility to its own. The relationship of Christians as brothers and sisters in Christ implies a commitment to serve and to care for one another. This was Paul's concern when he instructed Timothy about the church's duty to care for widows. The support of widows who had no one to care for them was an opportunity for the household of faith at Ephesus to express concretely a loving concern for its own and to share, as a family, material resources.

The family and church are closely bound together. Members of a family have mutual responsibilities. The same holds true in the household of faith. As we might expect, Paul not only pointed out the duties of the church to the widows but also the duties of the widows to the church.

I. Responsibilities of Christians (5:3-8)

Among the believers at Ephesus were widows who had no means of supporting themselves. Caring for these persons was one of the ministries of the church. At Jerusalem the Seven were appointed so that the widows might not be neglected (Acts 6:1-6). Apparently a number of the widows in the Ephesian church were unable to get gainful employment and had no opportunity for marriage. Their only source of financial support was the church. Paul's discussion of the problem began with a statement of the Christians' responsibilities in this matter.

A. To Assist the Needy in the Church (5:3-6)

The words of Paul here applied not only to Timothy but also to the whole church. He instructed the members to care for one another and bear one another's burdens. His directive was: "Give proper recognition [*timaō*, "show honor, give support"] to those widows who are really in need." This does not imply indifference to the needs of those outside the church. But the burden of the directive was that sisters under the same roof should not go hungry or be forced to dress in rags.[1] Material assistance was a way of expressing honor. The people on Malta gave gifts to Paul and his companions for bringing them the gospel. Luke took note of their gratitude when he wrote, "They honored us in many ways" (Acts 28:10). Giving assistance or bestowing gifts is one way of expressing recognition and honor.

As Paul had indicated, the church had an obligation to provide

---

1. Paul F. Barackman, *The Epistles of Timothy and Titus,* p. 61.

for the widows with real needs. At the same time he warned against the selfish and the indolent. Evidently some widows were tempted to impose on the church's generosity and to avoid their own responsibilities. The apostle wanted to guard against this and to encourage sound economy in the household of faith. Therefore he gave two directives.

1. The church was not to give assistance to widows with families. Children were not to abandon their parents or grandparents. Providing support for these people would have been an additional burden for the church. The congregation did not have an abundance of material wealth, but the real reason was that the children "should learn first of all to put their religion into practice by caring for their own family and so repaying their parents and grandparents." Religious devoutness at church is no substitute for the proper care of parents. The fifth commandment requires children to honor parents. Adequate provision for aged parents is an important part of obeying this commandment.

Children have received much from their parents. They owe their parents a great deal. It is only natural for them to be concerned with their parents' welfare. Today pensions are provided to relieve the young people of the burden. But even when there is no economic necessity, the basic obligation remains. Older people have many needs that financial support fails to satisfy. For the children to discharge their obligation requires more than material support.

2. The church should not assist widows who think only of pleasure. Among the widows were those who had no claim to the support of the church. Their lifestyles were not in keeping with the teaching of Christ. As Paul wrote, "But the widow who lives for pleasure is dead even while she lives." The pursuit of pleasure and luxurious and riotous living were evidence that a widow was only a nominal Christian. Physically she was still living, but spiritually she was dead.[2] She chose a fast life rather

---

2. The force of the perfect tense (*tethnēken*) indicates that the widow had died and was continuing in a state of death.

than a life in Christ. She was dead to God and stood in contrast to the widow who put her hope in Christ and continued "night and day to pray and to ask God for help."

One observation needs to be made here. The life of the church is similar to family life. Those who are not members of a family cannot expect to share the family benefits. Persons living indolently and giving themselves to pleasure have no claim on the church's care. They live in death. They do not in any real sense belong to the church and must not be allowed to become parasites on it.

B. To Provide for the Needs of the Household
   (5:7–8)

Instructions also were offered to the families of widows so that they might be without blame. Those who allowed their relatives to be dependent on the church were more to blame than their dependents. They were not to abandon their needy relatives such as parents or grandparents. The Christian duty was to provide for them according to their needs.

However, the care of the immediate family was even more binding on the believer. Unbelievers made proper provision for their families. Common decency demanded such, and it also was an indisputable Christian duty. The believer who neglected his needy relatives, especially members of his own household, had denied the faith.

The very heart of the gospel is to love all men. A man who neglects his own family has no part in the gospel. He has failed to do what the law of love demands. He has not measured up to the best pagan standard in regard to his family. He "is worse than an unbeliever." In fact, he is "worse" (*cheirōn*) than a person who knows nothing about Christ's marvelous example of love. His spiritual condition is worse than that of a person who makes no claim to know the saving power of Christ. The true believer is to labor to provide for himself and for those of his family who are dependent on him. It is a mark of integrity and a fruit of the Spirit of Christ.

II. Widows in the Service of the Church
(5:9-10)

Evidently the church at Ephesus had an official list of widows. The Greek word (*katalegō*) was used for being placed on a recognized list. Who were the widows who were placed on the list? Were they deaconesses or assistants to the deacons? Or were they only the widows who were genuinely destitute and had no one to support them but the church? There is no way of being certain. The qualifications listed in verses 9 and 10 could have been for the purpose of keeping to a minimum the number of widows receiving support from the church. The church at Ephesus was not likely to have had an abundance of material goods. However, it is quite possible that these qualifications were applied to widows who had a spiritual ministry in the church. They must have devoted their time to Christian work and were not widows in the ordinary sense. The qualifications that they had to satisfy leave no doubt that they were selected carefully.

Consider now the very practical qualifications for the order of widows.

A. Sixty Years Old or Older (5:9a)[3]

At this age a widow probably would not remarry. A widow who was sixty or more years old would have been an experienced person; the possibility of her remarrying would have been greatly reduced. She would not have had the responsibilities of a husband and children and would have had the experience and the time to render valuable assistance. She could devote her time to caring for orphans, to visiting and praying for the sick, and to other forms of ministry. Setting the age at sixty or older was probably a safeguard against remarriage, and at that age the widow would have little desire to take up worldly pleasures and interests. Distractions from giving herself full time to the ministry of the church would have been diminished.

---

3. Verse 9a in The New International Version reads, "No widow may be put on the list of widows unless she is over sixty." The word "over" (*elatton*) in this version is more accurately rendered "less than." No widow less than sixty years old was to be placed on the list.

It cannot be assumed that the church refused to help widows under sixty. Younger widows with children would have had the greatest needs. For the church to have arbitrarily denied them support would have been cruel. The special qualifications, including the age restriction, were required only of widows who devoted themselves wholly to the work of the church.

B. Faithful to Her Husband (5:9b)

The literal translation of this requirement is "the woman of one man." Apparently the phrase means that she had been a faithful wife.[4] The marriage bond was lightly regarded in the ancient world. Men and women changed partners quickly. Any widow who gave herself to Christian work was required to have been faithful to her husband. Moral integrity has always been fundamental to Christian service and life.

Marrying again after the death of a woman's first husband was not likely a disqualification. Paul advised the young widows to remarry (5:14). Barring a woman from the list of widows at the death of a second husband would have been unfair. It is not very likely that she would have been penalized for something Paul advised her to do.

C. Commitment to a Life of Service (5:10)

A good reputation was important. Before a widow was enrolled, sufficient evidence was required that she had devoted herself to the service of others. Good works must have been part of her daily works and life. The church was to be cautious in enrolling a widow. Only the widow who demonstrated, through noble deeds, a disposition for the work was to be placed on the list. Paul listed four areas in which she must have excelled in good works.

1. Reared children. The widow must have had some experience in child care and rearing. Most women sixty years old

---

4. Donald Guthrie, *The Pastoral Epistles,* (Tyndale New Testament Commentaries), p. 102, understands the requirement to be that the widow not remarry after the death of her husband. People in the ancient world esteemed widows who refrained from a second marriage. The prophetess Anna is an example (Luke 2:36).

would have had children of their own.[5] Because of that kind of experience a widow would have been able to give valuable counsel to the younger women in the church. Having reared her family in the Christian way, she would be able to impart information about spiritual as well as physical care. Instructing the younger women as to how they might rear their families was a real opportunity for ministry.

The Christian family and home are under attack today. God has given some believers the gift or the aptitude to minister to torn families and homes. The need is great for these gifted servants to apply the healing and reconciling grace of the gospel to situations of conflict and alienation.

2. *Showed hospitality to strangers.* The entertaining of strangers was usually the duty of the woman. Widows known for their kindness in providing for the needs of Christian strangers were a blessing to the church. Many of the early Christians traveled. A Christian family on a journey would need lodging. Those rendering valuable service for the church, such as preachers and teachers, would need a place to stay. "Inns in the ancient world were notoriously dirty, notoriously expensive, and notoriously immoral."[6] It must have been common for Christian travelers to seek out those of the faith for fellowship and shelter. The widow devoted to the work of the church had to be a woman of hospitality. Her home could not be a home where the doors were barred against the need of others. She had to be willing to share the comfort of her home with others and minister to the needs of those beyond her own family. Some of the happiest Christian homes are those where doors are open to the needs of others and where a hospitable spirit prevails.

3. *Washed the saints' feet.* The washing of feet occupied a significant place in Eastern hospitality. It was a custom to wash the feet of a guest after a dusty journey. Often it was the responsibility of a slave to wash a person's feet. Because of this, a

---

5. Some biblical scholars take this to imply that the widow must have reared a child abandoned by his parents. Nothing is said about orphans.
6. William Barclay, *The Letters to Timothy, Titus and Philemon,* p. 128.

prominent interpretation of this verse has been that the Christian widow was to be willing to perform the humblest of tasks in the service of Christ. However, Paul specifically indicates that she must have washed the saints' feet. She must have washed the feet of God's people, just as Jesus had commanded His disciples (John 13). She must have shown herself to be a servant of the servants of God. The washing of the saints' feet would be evidence of her dedication to Christ and her willingness to obey Him.

Possibly more is intended than merely the widow's spiritual aptitude.[7] It could have been a sign of her standing in the community of Christ. She stood in a right relationship with the community of believers. Or to put it another way, she reflected in washing the saints' feet the servant nature of the Christian life. By washing others' feet she demonstrated that she was sincere and worthy of the support of the church. So her washing of the saints' feet was more than a menial task. It had redemptive significance, portraying the servanthood of Jesus Christ and serving as a reminder of the continual cleansing through the suffering and death of Christ.

4. Helped those in trouble. None of the particulars of the nature of the trouble are given. One possibility is that this refers to the care of the sick and the poor; the church must maintain a loving concern for the afflicted and needy. Another possibility is that this meant ministering to those persecuted for their faith and in prison. Persecution of the early Christians was common. To offer the persecuted help was to identify with them and to

---

7. The exact significance of washing the saints' feet is hard to determine. One fact that militates against understanding it simply as a sign of hospitality is that it is part of the catalogue of requirements. Since hospitality is explicitly mentioned in the list, the significance of washing the saints' feet may be deeper than hospitality extended in humility. The phrase "saints' feet" adds a new dimension to the concept and implies that the practice of washing feet had special significance within the Christian community. As to why this was required of only the widows and apparently not of the overseer-elder or the deacon is difficult to ascertain. Chris Thomas is preparing a doctoral dissertation on the account in John 13 of Jesus' washing the disciples' feet. The study will examine the Jewish and Hellenistic backgrounds of washing feet and will address the theological concerns raised by this practice in the church.

also risk persecution and imprisonment. Believers must minister to those who suffer for their faith, even if in doing so it brings trouble on them.

To have been placed on the list of widows required dedication "to all kinds of good deeds." What a tremendous value are such people to the household of faith! Their diligent pursuit of all good works singles them out as special servants of the church and provides a noble example for all Christians to follow.

III. Concern for the Good Name of the Church (5:11-16)

The church at Ephesus had suffered reproach because of the actions of certain people. This prompted the admonition: "give the enemy no opportunity for slander"; but Paul went on to observe that "some have in fact already turned away to follow Satan." What some of the widows had done had undermined the reputation of the church and had played into the hands of Satan. The desire to uphold the good name of the church should have prompted them to a strong commitment to the Christian life.

It was sad that the character of some of the widows in the church was open to serious question. Their improper conduct was not a matter of mere hearsay, nor was it without foundation. They had followed after Satan and had become his servants. Their conduct, which Paul alluded to in verse 13, gave the opponents of Christianity an opportunity to slander the church. Scandal marred the good name of the church, the household of God. Inevitably the honor of God's family suffers when those in the family fall into sin. So Paul sought to correct a situation that involved some of the young widows at Ephesus and to enhance the reputation of the church in the outside world.

A. Widows of Marriageable Age (5:11-15)

Among the widows were those under sixty. They were not to be consecrated to the order of widows. Much of the work of those placed on the official list required experience and complete devotion.

1. A pledge. At the time of enrollment the widow pledged to devote herself to the service of the church. Apparently the commitment was for life. At least the work was such that it required wholehearted devotion. That kind of dedication was too much for most of the young widows and could have become very distressing. Likely they would have found themselves torn between serving in a spiritual ministry and looking for a prospective husband. Under those conditions they could not have discharged their duties to the church and would have remarried should they have had the opportunity.

Because of this a young widow was not to be placed on the list of widows. Those on the list apparently were required to devote most of their time to the ministry of the church. The demands of the church were too great for them to assume the responsibilities that go with marriage and a family. But it was natural and normal for a young widow to remarry. She was not condemned for remarrying. What was condemned is breaking a vow. A young woman's husband might have died. Out of impulse she could have decided not to remarry and to devote herself to the work of the church. She would have pledged to refrain from a second marriage and to give herself wholeheartedly to the service of the church. Consequently she would have been consecrated to the order of widows. But later she took the opportunity to marry again and forsook her sacred obligation to serve the church.

Marriage is a natural state and celibacy is demanded of none. Normally nothing would have been wrong with a young widow remarrying. However, by doing so, she broke her pledge to remain single. Having taken a vow, her obligation was to be true to it.

Paul knew that many young widows would become restless. The wish to marry again would distract them from the faithful discharge of their duties to the church. Their desire for marriage would have "overcome their dedication to Christ." The consequences of breaking their vows would be serious—"they bring judgment on themselves." The rendering of "judgment" (*krima*) as "damnation" is too strong. The reference is not to the final judgment. "Bring" (*echousai*) is present tense and does not refer to future judgment. The meaning is that widows who broke their sacred pledge in order to marry again would be deserving of censure.[8] They would bring on themselves reproach "because they have broken their first pledge." It was not a matter of setting aside their original faith in Christ but of their pledge to do the work of the church. As a result they involved themselves in judgment, that is, guilt for being untrue to their pledge.

The apostle had the interests of the young widows at heart. He wanted to spare their being condemned for faithlessness. Thus he recommended that they not be enrolled at all and should be given the right to remarry.

2. A danger. Some of the young widows had fallen into the peril of idleness. Their bad habits caused the good name of the church to suffer.

Idleness had two unfortunate results. These widows went from house to house. The young widows were prone to become restless. Because they did not have enough to do, they drifted from house to house and abused their privileges of visitation. They became gadabouts.

Part of the widows' work in the church could have very well been home visitation and would have provided them with an excuse for going around from house to house. They could have very easily turned their ministry into a social affair. No doubt this is a peril for many Christian workers, especially for those who devote most of their time to the work of the ministry and also enjoy companionship. The turning of our ministry into a mere social affair dissipates it and nullifies its impact.

The second result was that these widows became "gossips and busybodies, saying things they ought not to." Such women became chatty, loose talkers and busybodies, meddling in the affairs of others, rather than busy workers. Their conversation degenerated into gossip. They babbled whatever came into their minds and made empty charges and false accusations. They repeated tales and scandal from house to house. Each time they perhaps added a little something to the gossip, making it, as talebearers and scandalmongers do, more malicious and cruel.

---

8. Guthrie, *The Pastoral Epistles,* (Tyndale New Testament Commentaries), p. 103.

Exactly why Paul understood that the younger widows were more prone to fall into this peril than the older ones is not clear. But their personal interest in others had gone wrong. Of course, every Christian is to be concerned about the affairs of others. No Christian is to turn his interest in on himself and live a life that shuts out the concerns of others. When love is absent, busying ourselves about the affairs of other people becomes malicious and even cruel at times. All Christians should guard themselves against becoming "gossips and busybodies, saying things they ought not to."

What is the best way to avoid falling into this peril? The answer is in genuine love—love that is shed abroad in our hearts by the Holy Spirit. The Spirit directs us to speak only the truth and to speak it only in love. He directs us to be concerned about the affairs of others. Such concern is to be in love so that it is not merely meddling in the affairs of others.

3. *A recommendation.* The apostle had a real concern for the young widows in the Ephesian church. He urged the young widows to marry again. In 1 Corinthians 7:39 he gave the same advice to widows with one condition—that they marry "in the Lord." To put it another way, their husbands were to be Christians. This was advice. The fact that he was not commanding them to remarry is reflected in the translation: "I counsel [*boulomai*, "will, desire"] younger widows to marry."

For these young widows marriage was desirable for two reasons. First, they could occupy themselves with the concerns of a home. The responsibility of making a home would have been conducive to their happiness and would have allowed them to fulfill their natural calling in bearing children. This calling is one of the highest and is divinely ordained. Indeed the task of rearing a family and making a home is a noble and great responsibility. God must be delighted when His maidservants are faithful to this ministry and make Christ dominant in their homes.

The young widows were advised to remarry for a second reason. It would prevent them from giving an enemy opportunity for slander. Here the word "enemy" does not refer specifically to Satan but to any unbeliever who sets himself over against the church.[9] The desire was that the young women not fall into temptation. When that happened, it gave an adversary an opportunity to criticize the church. The sins of Christians still bring reproach on themselves and dishonor on the name of God. The enemies of Christ are swift to use scandal among the members of God's family to discredit the church and its message.

The church at Ephesus had suffered as a result of some of its members' conduct. Among the young widows were some who had followed Satan rather than Christ. By their improper conduct they had turned aside from the path of righteousness and compromised the ethical demands of the gospel. They had played into the hands of the enemy. A genuinely Christian life is a powerful witness to the truth of the gospel, but the cause of Christ is greatly hindered when professing Christians depart from the way of holiness.

B. Care for Needy Widows (5:16)

The apostle expressed concern about the conduct of the young widows, but he also desired that provision be made for the care of needy widows. The question was who should assume this responsibility. Was the congregation or a relative of a destitute mother or grandmother to assume this burden? Note Paul's directives.

1. The Christian family. If a Christian woman had an aged widow in her home, she was to provide for her needs. Where there was a needy widow in a Christian household, the wife was responsible for her welfare. Such a widow had no way of earning a livelihood. Assisting a widow in need would have been pleasing to God. God's heart has always gone out to the poor and the oppressed, and to the widow and the fatherless. Christians have a moral responsibility to provide for those of their own household.

2. The church. The widows who were without relatives were to receive assistance from the church. Apparently the reason

---

9. The form is a present participle of the verb *antikeimai*, which means "to lie against, to oppose, to be an adversary."

was that the church was not able to support all who came for aid. The congregation's financial resources must have been limited. Christian families were to provide for their own widows and not shift that burden to the household of faith. The support of the church was to be reserved for the destitute. They were left alone with no one but the church to provide for them. Many churches' material resources are limited and these churches are able to provide only for those who have no other source of help.

IV. Conclusion

Out of Paul's discussion of the treatment of widows emerge three truths that are never out of date. First, as a family, the church is obligated to care for the material welfare of its members who have genuine needs. The household of God, the extended family, must show special concern and compassion for the widows, the orphans, the poor, and the oppressed in its midst. Pastoral care includes more than simply spiritual nurture of all church members. It also requires providing for the material needs of brothers and sisters in the Lord (James 2:15f.; 1 John 3:17f.).

The church is to be more than just a believing community. It is to be a caring family that exercises generosity toward its members who have economic needs. From its earliest days the church at Jerusalem felt a responsibility to look after its poor members (Acts 2:44f.), and in just a short time seven men were appointed to care specifically for this ministry (Acts 6:1–8). Paul also encouraged the churches he established to give to the poor Christians in Palestine (Rom. 15:27; 2 Cor. 8:9). The people of God have no right to turn their backs on needy members of the household of faith. Where the resources are sufficient, the church also does well in aiding the disadvantaged outside of the community of believers.

Second, the Christian family that has those who are unable to provide for themselves has a responsibility for their welfare. The church is to help those who have no one to help them, but the church's generosity is not an excuse for children to evade their responsibility for aged parents. It is the duty of children, according to Paul, to support their dependent parents. A man owes a special debt to those who gave him birth and brought him up. For him to care for his parents when they are old is pleasing to God.

Providing for the aged can be a real burden, but it is a burden that a Christian family should bear. Pensions and other retirement benefits do much to relieve this burden. Aged parents have other needs, even if there is no economic necessity. Whatever their dependents' needs are, the Christian family is to discharge its obligation to its own. The family of God is to use some of its resources to assist those who have no one to look to but the church.

Third, of significant importance is the opinion that the outside world has of the household of faith. The good name of a family depends on the character of its members. Nothing can mar more the reputation of the household of God than for some of its members to be guilty of scandal. The outside world does not hesitate to use scandal to discredit the church.

The individual member must not give opportunity for the world to criticize the church. Professing Christians who fail to keep their word and vows and fall into immorality bring not only themselves but also the church into disrepute. Their integrity in word and their integrity in conduct are vital to the good name of the household of faith.

9

Fidelity to True Religion

(6:3–10, 17–19)

False doctrine is a serious matter. When the gospel is distorted, men are offered something that will not meet their needs. The Christian preacher and teacher have been entrusted with "the word of truth." What they preach or teach is bound to affect others. The distortion of the truth does men spiritual harm.

Timothy had received "the word of truth," the apostolic faith, from Paul. He was to communicate the message to others, giving an accurate and plain exposition of the truth. He was not to falsify it, corrupt it, or add to it; but as Paul instructed his young associate:

> Do your best to present yourself to God as one approved, a workman who does not need to be ashamed and who correctly handles the word of truth. Avoid godless chatter, because those who indulge in it will become more and more ungodly. Their teaching will spread like gangrene. [2 Tim. 2:15–17]

Like all preachers and teachers, Timothy was to handle the word of truth with scrupulous care. He was to avoid confusing people, as Elymas the sorcerer had done by "perverting the right ways of the Lord" (Acts 13:10). The faithful proclamation of God's truth makes it easy for others to follow and ministers to their spiritual needs.

At Ephesus the false teachers were substituting doctrines that did not agree with "the sound instruction" and "godly teaching."

They had "an unhealthy interest in controversies and arguments." These people were teaching serious error. So Paul again drew attention to some of the perils threatening Timothy and the church. His emphasis was twofold: the character of the false teachers and the evil effects of what they did.

I. The Character of True Religion (6:3)

False teachers had invaded the church. The desire of these people was to press their own views and ideas on the Christians. Again Paul directed Timothy about how to deal with heretical teachers and unsound doctrine. To begin with, he defined the nature of true doctrine.

A. Sound Instruction (6:3a)

Literally "sound instruction" is "healthy words." Elsewhere Paul called such instruction "the whole will of God" (Acts 20:27). The divine message, which made the whole of God's will plain, consists of "sound instruction." The word *sound (hugiainō)* is used in the Gospels when speaking of people whom Jesus healed. Previously these people had been lame and diseased. Now they were sound or whole.

This involved more than physical well-being. A more profound healing took place through meeting Jesus. A person was healed in his entire being by the word of the Savior (John 7:23), that is, saved from his sin (Luke 5:21f.). An example of this truth is when the prodigal returned to the home of his father. He was "safe and sound" (*hugiainō*, Luke 15:27). His physical well-being could not account fully for what happened to him. Something much deeper transpired. The lost son's alienation had been put away, and he had been restored to his father's home. Therefore the message of the parable of the prodigal is this: When a person encounters the heavenly Father, he is made spiritually whole and restored to full health.

The reconciling, healing power of the Christian faith attests that it is sound instruction. Indeed the message of Jesus consists of sound words because it is not diseased but whole—the whole counsel of God that provides spiritual life and health. The counsel of God sets forth truth about God in His holiness and love, about man as a sinner in need of saving grace, about the Savior who delivers man from his plight, and about demands of the gospel for an upright life and, therefore, is wholesome and crucial to a vigorous spiritual life.

It is unclear whether the expression "sound instruction of our Lord" means words spoken by Jesus Himself or truth about Him.[1] Both meanings are good, but "sound instruction concerning the Lord" may be more fitting. E. F. Scott recognizes that either meaning is possible, but makes this observation:

> Paul invariably thinks of the message concerning Christ when he speaks of the 'word' or 'gospel'; and the allusion to 'healthy words' would likewise suggest words which deal with the right subject, not with vain abstractions, but with Christ Himself.[2]

B. Godly Teaching (6:3b)

The fruit of sound instruction is sober living. Such living is reflected in humility and reverence toward God and in a useful life. To put it another way, doctrine uninfected by men's speculations and free of human corruptions cultivates and produces godliness. Sound doctrine edifies the body of Christ and builds up the believer's faith in Christ.

In short, the aim of true religion is godliness. What the false teachers at Ephesus advocated did not tally with "sound instruction" and was not in accord with what is described as "godly teaching" or, more literally, "doctrine that is according to godliness." They tampered with godly teaching and refused to give assent to it. They were peddling doctrines as dangerous to the soul as blood poisoning is to the body, destroying the church rather than edifying it, and denying the claims of true religion rather than promoting truth conducive to godly living. What they taught led people away from God and led them more and more into ungodliness.

---

1. "Sound instruction of our Lord" can be either a subjective genitive (teachings that Jesus uttered during His earthly ministry) or an objective genitive (truths about Jesus).

2. *The Pastoral Epistles,* (The Moffatt New Testament Commentary), p. 73.

II. The Characteristics of Perverters of True Religion (6:4-5)

A description of a teacher can reveal much about the nature of his teaching. This is evident in Paul's picture of the false teachers. The characteristics of these people make it clear that their message was mistaken and misleading. The apostle singled out the characteristic marks of the false teachers.

A. Conceited and Ignorant (6:4a)

Literally "conceited" (*tetuphōtai*) means "has been filled with smoke." Those people were puffed up and proud. They had inflated egos and minds beclouded by their own conceits. They were too impressed with themselves and their own understanding. Being blinded by pride, they did not realize their ignorance. They knew nothing, yet they thought of themselves as wise people. Frequently pride and ignorance go hand in hand.

The temptation is great for the Christian worker to think more highly of himself than he ought. Anyone who stands before a congregation Sunday after Sunday or who regularly teaches the Word of God can become wrapped up in his own conceit. When that happens, he puts himself rather than Christ on display. Truth is sacrificed for the praise of men. The people are encouraged to follow the preacher or the teacher rather than Christ.

B. Morbid Love for Controversy (6:4b-5b)

The heretics had what Paul called "an unhealthy interest in controversies and arguments." Here the word "controversies" (*zētēseis*) is coupled with "arguments" (*logomachiai*), meaning "word battles." Normally the singular of "controversies" signifies either "investigations," such as the charges against Paul that Festus told King Agrippa he was at a loss to investigate (Acts 25:20) or the "debate" that occurred over circumcision (Acts 15:2). The former meaning suggests investigation that is philosophical in nature; the latter involves debate over an issue that is controversial.

Both meanings are common in the Pastoral Epistles. Paul

warned Timothy not to have anything to do with "stupid arguments (*zēteseis*), because . . . they produce quarrels" (2 Tim.
2:23). Titus was instructed to avoid four things: "foolish controversies (*zēteseis*) and genealogies [speculations] and arguments
and quarrels about the law" (Titus 3:9). The false teachers no
doubt had a love for philosophical speculation and for controversy. Their minds were sick because they had an unhealthy
interest in certain questions. They had rejected the sound words
of Jesus. The result was sickness—an insane preoccupation with
intellectual trifles and a morbid interest in heated arguments.
The insignificant was blown up to be the most important.

Arguments and glib speculations contribute little to the Christian life. An expert in subtle questions may be impressive and
able to destroy his opponent, but the outcome of controversies
and word battles are clear symptoms of moral sickness. The
evil results of such are listed.

*1. "Envy" (*phthonos*).* Heated arguing about words brings
about jealousy. That kind of exchange ordinarily produces a
winner and a loser. The loser is usually humiliated and suffers
the loss of admirers and prestige. As a result he becomes
envious of the victor's following and recognition.

*2. "Quarreling" (*eris, "strife"*).* This results when the loser
refuses to accept defeat. The debate degenerates into wrangling,
bitter conflict, and ill will. The opponents contradict and denounce one another.

*3. "Malicious talk" (*blasphēmiai, "railings"*).* The word literally
means "blasphemies" and refers here to abusive language.
When this occurs, those engaging in debate have nothing but
disdain and contempt for each other. They cannot stand for
their theological or philosophical positions to be challenged.
Therefore, they resort to slander and insults, not having learned
to speak in love.

*4. "Evil suspicions" (*huponoiai ponērai*).* Mistrust is implied
by this phrase. The actions and the motives of the opponent are
suspect. This is a sickness and can spread like cancer as evil
suspicions make their way into the mind. The outcome can be
that no one is trusted.

141

5. *"Constant friction"* (diaparatribai, *"mutual rubbing or irritation"*). As men argue, they constantly rub one another the wrong way. They find themselves given to constant contention and incessant wrangling and strife. Such people disturb the peace of the church and stir up religious controversy.

All of these symptoms are the results of men of corrupt minds who are destitute of the truth. Though they have the mental capacity to think about the higher things of life, their minds are depraved and devoid of truth. Minds of false teachers thrive on falsehoods. With their minds deprived of truth, these people have lost sight of reality. They have an intellectual curiosity about trifles but have no use for the truth revealed in Jesus Christ.

C. Considered Godliness As a Source of Gain (6:5c)

The minds of the Ephesian heretics were so depraved that they commercialized religion—imagining that "godliness is a means to financial gain." The apostle understood that Christians who devoted themselves to ministry were worthy of their hire. The false teachers did not look on preaching and teaching as a vocation but as a career. For them religion was a business—a means of promoting themselves.

Did the false teachers charge large fees for instruction or did they think that the outward practice of religion would get them a promotion or a social position? Which was true we cannot be certain, but as Scott says,

> The general meaning is plain, but it is doubtful whether the religion in question is their own or that of others. Do they use the piety of their neighbours in order to make money out of them? Or do they cultivate a pious mode of life for the sake of profit? Both kinds of religious imposture have been familiar in every age; but the words that follow would seem to point to the second meaning. The false teachers are to all appearance religious, but behind their religion there is a sordid and earthly motive. Perhaps the reference is to the fees they demanded (after the manner of philosophical tutors of the time) in return for religious instruction. Or the meaning may be more general. A reputation for high religious character has always been an asset for the man who aims at worldly power and

success; one has only to think of financiers and politicians of our own time who have learned that secret.[3]

Exactly how religion was a paying concern is uncertain, but this much is clear—the false teachers were out for gain. They were preaching and teaching to advance themselves. The true servant of Christ is not in the ministry for what he can get out of it. His motive is to be spent in the service of God and his fellow man.

III. The Reward and the Antithesis of True Religion (6:6-10)

True religion yields rewards, but they do not depend on earthly gains or circumstances. The plea is not for poverty. Being poor does not guarantee virtue, but Paul did point out that wealth is not fundamental to true happiness.

A. Godliness with Contentment (6:6–8)

Significant here is the word "contentment" (*autarkeia*). It means "self-sufficiency, a contented spirit." Such a sense of inner satisfaction springs from godly piety or a genuine devotion to God and is the result of having peace with God and fellowship with Christ. The blessings that come with godly living bring real contentment. Neither poverty nor wealth determines it. "I have learned the secret of being content," wrote Paul, "in any and every situation, whether well fed or hungry, whether living in plenty or in want" (Phil. 4:12). That kind of satisfaction does not come from the possession of external things. True religion creates contentment with what we have, but it does have its rewards.

1. Godliness is the means of "great gain." There are preachers who think that godliness and material gain are the same. Prosperity is no sure sign of godliness. Nor is godliness a guarantee of affluence. However, godliness is profitable. With

---

3. Ibid., p. 74.

contentment godliness is great gain. In fact, it is freedom from anxiety about material possessions. Also, the inner resources of godliness can be depended on regardless of circumstances.

2. *Godliness is the means of the Christian fulfilling his vocation.* Wealth is not essential to man's well-being. He comes into the world with no possessions, and he makes his departure the same way. The acquisition of goods is only temporary. Man comes and departs empty-handed. "Naked came I out of my mother's womb," Job declared, "and naked shall I return" (1:21, KJV).

Wealth is not evil. Being rich is not wrong. But the desire for riches is a peril for the Christian. He is to be content with the necessities of life—food and clothing.[4] His calling is not to pursue mammon. The only way a Christian fulfills his vocation is by the pursuit of godliness. Jesus said, "Seek first his [God's] kingdom and his righteousness" (Matt. 6:33). Paul urged Timothy to "pursue righteousness, godliness, faith, love, endurance and gentleness" (6:11). The pursuit of these is the vocation of every believer. God's call is a summons to devotion and to the supreme concerns of life and eternity.

B. Passion for Riches (6:9–10)

The strong desire for wealth is a great enemy of true religion. Any person possessed by this desire is in grave danger. Greed has a number of devastating results.

1. *Greed causes men to fall into temptation.* Passion for things can be a driving force in a man's life. When he is controlled by greed, he can easily be led to do wrong to acquire possessions. He may be tempted to resort to shady means and deals to get them. Doubtless men are led to many temptations by the desire to become rich.

2. *Greed causes men to fall into "a trap"* (pagis, "snare"). Animals are lured into traps, but men can fall into a trap set by the devil. The truth is that those consumed by the desire for

---

4. The term *raiment* (*skepasma*) is a general word and can also refer to shelter.

riches are already in the devil's trap. He uses their insatiable passion for riches to entangle and to imprison them. They are victims and captives of the devil. Like those mentioned in 2 Timothy 2:26, they need to "come to their senses and escape from the trap of the devil, who has taken them captive to do his will."

3. *Greed causes men to become prey to many evil desires.* An ungodly passion breeds other such desires. An eye for only riches leads to "many foolish and harmful desires." A person with a passionate love of mammon inevitably longs for ease, popularity, and sumptuous living. These kinds of desires are "foolish and harmful." They are foolish because reason cannot justify such passions. They are harmful because such passions destroy character. Gratification of them forfeits true joy and blessedness.

4. *Greed causes men to lose their faith.* The pursuit of gain "plunge[s] [*buthizō*, "submerges, drowns"] men into ruin and destruction." The words "ruin" and "destruction" may express "loss here and loss hereafter," but they very definitely include the idea of eternal ruin and punishment. The passion for wealth does not lead to ultimate gain but to ultimate loss. The man who is possessed by this passion is on a sinking ship. Unless he abandons the ship, he will drown in a sea of ruin and will plunge into total loss in eternity. This is the climax of falling "into temptation and a trap and into many foolish and harmful desires." The desire for wealth plunges its victim into the sea of destruction. The loss is everlasting. The ruin is eternal. What is lost can never be recovered.

Many evils can be traced back to the craving for money or material things. To make that even clearer Paul declared, "The love of money is the root of all kinds of evil." It should not be thought that the love of money is the root of *all* evil. The passion for money is only one source of evil (cf. Heb. 12:15). Money in itself is neither good nor bad; it carries with it a great responsibility. However, coveting money leads to great temptations—to all kinds of evil. Judas betrayed the Lord for thirty pieces of silver. Ananias and Sapphira lied to the Holy Spirit about the proceeds from selling a piece of property. The love of money has resulted in cheating, robbery, and murder.

In Paul's day some aspired to be rich and wandered (literally, "were led astray") from the faith. They were deceived by the spirit of covetousness. Reaching out for money, they went astray from the faith. They suffered the worst of evils—spiritual disaster. As Paul stated, they also "pierced themselves with many griefs." It was as though they had thrust a sword into their own bodies. They brought on themselves great pains. Material gain did not bring them satisfaction, but the opposite—dissatisfaction, unrest, and a spiritual vacuum. They lost their faith. In reality they committed spiritual suicide and gave up what was truly good and lasting in life for a few material things.

IV. The Wealthy and the True Religion (6:17-19)

The early church had in its ranks some wealthy members as well as poor people and slaves. As has been noted, Paul condemned the lust for wealth. However, he did not condemn the rich nor did he recommend that they give away all of their wealth. But he did instruct the rich about the perils of wealth, pointed out its true source, and urged them to use their material things in a responsible way.

A. Spiritual Perils of Wealth (6:17a, b)

Wealth in itself is not evil, but there are perils into which "those who are rich in this present world" (literally, "in the now age") can easily fall. Two of these are specified.

1. Pride in possessions. Wealth can easily lead to high-mindedness. Because of their material possessions the rich may think of themselves as better than other people. They may assume that their superior abilities are the reason for their success. They may view their prosperity as evidence of divine favor, but at the same time feel that they deserve it. Because they are materially secure, they may develop pride toward life and live as though they can chart their own destiny without any regard for God. There is nothing in this present age that gives a Christian the right to have a haughty spirit and to look down upon others. Least of all should worldly possessions lead a Christian to think that he is better than other members of the household of faith.

2. Trust in earthly possessions. What the world calls wealth will pass away as part of this present age. True riches cannot be found in material wealth. Those who place their trust in wealth have an unwarranted sense of security. Hope fixed on earthly possessions has no sure anchor. One thing that is certain is the uncertainty of riches. A person may be rich today and a pauper tomorrow. Only in God can man place his hope and let it rest there with absolute certainty that he will not be disappointed.[5] God can be counted on, but nothing is more uncertain in this unstable world than wealth.

B. Source of All Good Things (6:17c)

All the good things of the world are gifts from the hands of the Creator. Material things are not evil but good. They are blessings from the Giver of all things. God "richly provides us with everything for our enjoyment." The apostle who wrote these words knew what it was like to be in need, to go hungry, and to be without adequate clothing and shelter (Phil. 4:12; 2 Cor. 6:4; 11:27). He did not live in affluence and could have complained about the distribution of the good things in life, but he never did. He had learned to be content and satisfied. Whatever comes to a man's hand, whether little or much, is due to divine Providence and is intended for his pleasure. For the Christian the material things that he enjoys are to be reminders of the care of the heavenly Father, the bountiful Giver.

C. A Charge to the Wealthy (6:18-19)

Men with wealth have a great responsibility and opportunity to do good. By sharing wealth they are able to bring help and

---

5. The perfect (*ēlpikenai*) signifies "to have hope and continue to hope."

comfort to others. This is the emphasis of Paul in his two admonitions to the rich.

1. The wealthy are to be rich in good works. The hoarding of wealth enriches no one but the owner. A man with money can enrich others and do much good. He can minister to the physical needs of others and make their lives much easier. The best use of material gifts is in doing good. When riches are so used, no place is given to selfishness. A selfish person is a person with an impoverished soul. A generous person is a person rich in good works. Every person has the power to be rich in good deeds.

2. The rich are to be ready to contribute. People with wealth have a great opportunity to practice generosity. A person's generosity is judged by the use he makes of the good things of this world. Whether a person has little or much, he is to use what he has to serve spiritual life. As Paul reminded the rich, faithfulness in stewardship and a willingness to share bring lasting rewards.

Persons who are generous with what they have show that their desire is to please Christ and their perspective is eternal. There are two reasons for this. First, they lay up treasure for themselves in the coming age. No doubt they realize the folly of laying up treasure on the earth, since no one can take out of this world what he has accumulated. Because of their generosity they are decreasing their assets on earth, but at the same time they are increasing them in the world to come. By doing this they are laying "a firm foundation for the coming age." Wealth in itself is very uncertain, but by the proper use of it a good foundation is laid for the future. Such a foundation is firm and will endure in "the coming age." Second, they "take hold of the life that is truly life." True life is the life on which the Christian must set his heart. Life in this sense stands in contrast to life that is propped up by so uncertain a support as riches.[6] Life of the age to come is real life. Only in the hereafter can real life be received in its fullness, but even now the Christian can enjoy it.

---

6. Donald Guthrie, *The Pastoral Epistles*, (Tyndale New Testament Commentaries), p. 118.

V. Conclusion

All Christians are summoned to be faithful to true religion, which of course is encompassed in the gospel. From Paul's day to ours many believers have found it necessary "to contend for the faith that God has once for all entrusted to the saints" (Jude 3). So the false teachers at Ephesus have had their counterparts in every generation. They preach and teach not the gospel in its purity, but a distorted version of it. They are conceited and their ministry is designed not to serve God and man but themselves. They occupy themselves with "controversies and arguments," but their heated confrontations and glib theological speculations contribute little to living the Christian life. They disturb the peace of the church and commercialize religion, making their ministry a way of earning a living rather than a way of serving God. The platform of many such teachers is a gospel that guarantees peace of mind, health, and financial prosperity. Their doctrine does not agree with "the sound instruction" of Jesus Christ and with teaching that accords with godliness.

Every Christian needs to have an open mind. God may have yet more truth to break forth from His Word. Through the Holy Spirit God is still active in the world. The Spirit guides, illuminates, reproves, and empowers the people of God. Novelties in doctrine and new fads in theology have often proved to be doctrinal error and have failed to provide a solid basis for Christian faith and life. The apostle Paul's advice is still sound in regard to those who do not hold to wholesome doctrine (6:3-5). Any promptings of the Holy Spirit are to be tested by their conformity to the sound doctrines of Jesus Christ. If they do not conform, they are not in accord with the mind of Christ, disclosed in the Gospels and the Epistles of the New Testament; and they are not of the voice of the Spirit. Christ is the Way, the Truth, and the Life.

An error that is all too common and masquerades under the guise of true religion is that "godliness is a means to financial gain." Christian workers must receive a salary for their labor, but they are not to minister for the sake of the salary. A passion for money can destroy both a person's ministry and his relationship with God. To use the words of Paul, those "who want to get rich fall into temptation and a trap and into many foolish and harmful desires that plunge men into ruin and destruction." The apostle went on to say, "Some people, eager for money, have wandered from the faith and pierced themselves with many griefs." How could the consequences be otherwise? Lust for money and things is covetousness, and covetousness is idolatry. Godliness is not a means of gain. True religion is trust in God and its fruit is not covetousness but contentment. "Godliness with contentment is great gain. . . . If we have food and clothing, we will be content with that" (6:6, 8).

The grave danger is setting one's heart on riches. Wealth is not evil in itself. Having an abundance of earthly possessions is not wrong; but materialism, the love of things, is evil and is not consonant with the Spirit of grace. The poor as well as the rich can be gripped by materialism. Those who deal with a few dollars can fall into this trap of Satan as easily as those who deal with millions. In fact, among the rich are those who are very generous, but people who have little can become materialistic. Regardless of a person's economic level, he can be driven by the desire for a little more wealth.

God has blessed many Christians with financial prosperity. This can pose a real problem for believers. Material blessings are not bestowed in order that believers might selfishly serve their own desires. Such blessings are to be enjoyed, but they carry with them a great responsibility and a great opportunity for generous giving. Christians with wealth have the power to serve the needs of neighbors and to support the ministries of the church. They have the opportunity "to be rich in good deeds" and to "lay up treasure for themselves as a firm foundation for the coming age, so that they may take hold of the life that is truly life" (6:18, 19).

So the unselfish use of money and wealth is a source of great blessing. Poverty is not a virtue. Nothing is wrong with being rich as long as we are rich toward God. For many it is easier to be rich toward God when they have little than when they have much.

10

The Central Realities of the Faith

(6:11–16, 20–21)

The ravages of materialism are a constant danger for the people of God. However, they must be aware that the Christian life is not without other foes and that believers must "contend" against these foes if they are to conquer them and maintain the faith. Christians must lay hold on eternal life that they have received from Christ and live in the light of all its implications.

The apostle Paul knew that this demanded a strong commitment to the Christian faith. The kind of commitment that Paul urged had to be informed by the Word of God, which is normative for doctrine and practice. He did not fail to remind Timothy of this fact. These are some of his words to his young friend: "The holy Scriptures, . . . are able to make you wise for salvation through faith in Christ Jesus. All Scripture is God-breathed and is useful for teaching, rebuking, correcting and training in righteousness" (2 Tim. 3:15–16).

As a Christian leader Timothy was not only to expound the deepest truths of the Scriptures, but he also was to live by them. The central truths of the faith and the fundamental basis of Christian life and service are the sovereign majesty of God, the coming of Christ into the world, His sacrificial death·on the cross, His resurrection, the prospect of the final judgment, and life in the Spirit. These truths were the foundation on which

Paul urged Timothy to fight constantly "the good fight of the faith." Timothy entered into this fight when he became a believer; participation in the fight is required of all Christians.

I. A Christian Call to Strenuous Effort (6:11–12b)

Using an Old Testament title, the apostle addressed Timothy as "man of God." This was a title of respect and honor and was given to great leaders like Moses (Deut. 33:1), David (Neh. 12:24, 36), and Elisha (2 Kings 8:8). But the title itself simply means that a person belongs to God. In this sense every Christian is a man of God. However, it must have reminded Timothy not only of many of the Old Testament personalities who had borne the title but also of his responsibility in the church. He had been specifically called and equipped by the Holy Spirit for Christian service and thus was obligated to spare no effort to discharge his duties as a good soldier of Jesus Christ. To reinforce this, Paul renewed the call for Timothy to be faithful in the discharge of his ministry.

A. Flee (6:11a)

The exhortation is to "flee from all this" (literally, "these things"). In 2 Timothy 2:22 the young man is admonished to flee the evil desires of youth, but here the admonition seems to be broader and urges Timothy to avoid a wide assortment of vices.

As we consider this exhortation, it is important to note the term "flee" (*pheugō*). At times it defines flight from physical danger. Joseph was ordered to flee to Egypt with Mary and the infant Jesus (Matt. 2:13). When they were persecuted in one city, the disciples were to flee to the next and continue to preach the gospel (Matt. 10:23). Christians who were in Judea were commanded to flee to the mountains for safety when Jerusalem was in danger (Matt. 24:16; Luke 21:21).

The word also is used figuratively to signify a flight from spiritual danger. The Corinthians were told to flee from fornication (1 Cor. 6:18) and idolatry (10:14). Should a person flee (*apophengō*) from the evils of the world and then return to them, his subsequent spiritual condition is worse than his first entanglement (2 Peter 1:4; 2:18, 20).

Timothy was to flee from greedy ambitions and to shun sin. But all Christians need to recognize the grave danger that sin poses to their spiritual welfare. They are to be on constant alert against sin and get as far away from it as possible. There is no reason to be exposed to needless danger. Every Christian's faith will be tested, but each one must take care to avoid circumstances through which the enemy could lure him into sin.

B. Pursue (6:11b)

The verb "pursue" (*diōkō*) is the opposite of "flee" and literally means "to strive for, seek after, aspire to, prosecute." Frequently the term is used in connection with goals after which Christians must strive. In Romans 12:13, Christians are told to pursue hospitality and in Romans 14:19 they are instructed to pursue "what leads to peace and to mutual edification." 1 Corinthians 14:1 urges believers to pursue love, and 1 Thessalonians 5:15 exhorts them to pursue "that which is good" (KJV). Hebrews 12:14 admonishes them to pursue peace and holiness.

The Christian has a double duty. He is to "flee" and he is to "pursue." He must run away from spiritual danger, but he also must run after the spiritual life. With great persistence, he must separate himself from the old life and relentlessly pursue the new life in Jesus Christ.

The apostle explained to Timothy on what he was to set his heart. The noble qualities for which Timothy was to strive should be the aim of every Christian.

1. Righteousness (dikaiosunē). An examination of Scripture discloses that the term *righteousness* has a wide range of meanings. Divine righteousness is often associated with God's mighty saving acts. The death of Christ is the supreme saving act of God that reveals divine righteousness (Rom. 3:21–26). What was accomplished through Christ makes it possible for persons to be pardoned of their sin and accepted into a right relationship with God and then enabled to live a righteous life. Through Christ God took the initiative so that individuals could be set free from the power of sin. God's righteousness, God's mighty saving acts in the death and resurrection of Christ, offers the free gift of justification (Rom. 5:17).

Upon receiving this gift the individual is placed in a right relationship with God, but at the same time God bestows on him a new life (regeneration and sanctification) by the Holy Spirit. The person who appropriates God's righteousness, which is none other than God's grace in accepting and saving him, is to live a holy life. Standing in a right relationship with God, the Christian must be rightly related to God's will. His character and conduct must be right and pleasing to the heavenly Father.

This was Paul's emphasis in his charge to Timothy to "pursue righteousness." As E. F. Scott suggests, here the term *righteousness* can be rendered as "integrity."[1] The Christian is to aim at and strive for integrity. This demands "conformity to what is right towards both God and man."[2] A person of integrity renders to God and man what is due them.

2. Godliness (eusebeia). This has a similar meaning to the Old Testament phrase *fear of God* and basically indicates an attitude toward life. For the believers the attitude can never be divorced from Christ. The apostle did speak of "the knowledge of the truth that leads to godliness" (Titus 1:1) and of Christians who are to live "upright and godly lives in this present age" (Titus 2:12). But he understood that a godly life is lived in Christ (2 Tim. 3:12). The believer's devoutness is rooted and grounded in his union and fellowship with Jesus Christ. He lives his life in the presence of the Savior. Consciousness of this should have an impact on the entire attitude of the believer. A deep reverence for God and for all of life is the result and can be appropriately summed up in this one word, godliness—a personal quality that characterizes the life of the Christian who is keenly aware that he lives in the presence of God.

3. Faith (pistis). No New Testament author emphasizes faith more than Paul. For him "saving faith" receives what grace

---

1. *The Pastoral Epistles*, (The Moffatt New Testament Commentary), p. 76.
2. Donald Guthrie, *The Pastoral Epistles*, (Tyndale New Testament Commentaries), p. 114.

bestows. It relies on Jesus Christ as Savior and "puts Him on" for justification. Christ is the only object of saving faith.

However, faith is not a kind of passive resignation, since it issues in active obedience. Romans 1:5 speaks of "the obedience that comes from faith." The new life that the Christian enjoys begins with faith in Christ, but it continues with faith that manifests itself in obedience. The apostle's emphasis fell on what might be described as living faith or obedience when he urged Timothy to pursue faith. If a Christian heeds this directive, it means that he is faithful to the gospel regardless of the ups and downs in life. He remains loyal to God, even to the end.

*4. Love (*agapē*).* God is the author of love. By the Holy Spirit the love of God is poured out in the heart of the believer (Rom. 5:5). The supreme expression of God's love was in Jesus Christ (John 3:16). God's commending of His love toward men while they were still sinners (Rom. 5:6–8) was the basis of Paul's appeal for Timothy to pursue love.

Faith and love are frequently placed side by side (Eph. 6:23; 1 Thess. 1:3; 3:6; 5:8; 1 Tim. 1:14). In fact, faith is active in love (Gal. 5:6; 1 Thess. 3:6). When a person receives Christ, the love of God takes hold of him. He not merely is to be a believing person but also is to become a loving person. Apparently the apostle desired that Timothy become a loving servant of the gospel, loving both God and neighbor, loving even the teachers who were disseminating error at Ephesus.

"Love never fails" (1 Cor. 13:8). It is one of the most powerful forces. It holds the church together and builds it up (1 Cor. 8:1; Phil. 2:1f.; Col. 2:2; 2 Thess. 1:3). It impels Christian living and service. The law for the Christian is the law of love because he is to "do everything in love" (1 Cor. 16:14).

*5. "Endurance" (*hupomonē*).* Fundamental to the word "endurance" are ideas such as "steadfastness" and "constancy." A Christian with this personal quality is steady and lives a consistent life of righteousness, godliness, faith, love, and gentleness. He remains steadfast to the principles of the gospel and patiently endures trying circumstances and grievous adversities. Even in the greatest of trials and suffering he is constant and unswerving in his faith.

A passage in Romans 5 assures the believer that rejoicing in tribulation is in order because of the good results. According to verses 3–5, "we . . . rejoice in our sufferings, because we know that suffering produces perseverance (*hupomonē*); perseverance, character; and character, hope. And hope does not disappoint us." Near the end of Romans this admonition appears— "Be joyful in hope, patient (*hupomonē*) in affliction . . ." (12:12).

The Christian is urged to endure in the most trying of circumstances. "For everything that was written in the past was written to teach us, so that through endurance (*hupomonē*) and the encouragement of the Scriptures we might have hope" (Rom. 15:4). So endurance is closely tied to Christian hope. The truth is that "if we endure, we will also reign with him. If we disown him, he will also disown us" (2 Tim. 2:12).

As a man of God, Timothy was to make his target steadfastness in both the Christian life and service. This should be the aim of all Christians. Those who endure to the end will be saved (Matt. 24:13).

6. *"Gentleness"* (praupatheia). This quality is the opposite of sternness and harshness and can be described in terms of meekness, humility, and consideration. Alien to gentleness is the attitude that demands rights at all costs. Unbridled anger, brashness, and rudeness find no place in gentleness.

The character of our Lord was marked by meekness, humility, and consideration. Isaiah, in his description of the Servant of the Lord, anticipated so well Christ's attitude and life on earth. According to the prophet, the Servant gave His back to the smiters and His cheeks to them that plucked off the hair (50:6). He was despised and rejected of men, and one who was acquainted with great sorrow. Yet He never resisted or retaliated. Eventually He allowed Himself to be brought as a lamb to the slaughter, but even then He was as a sheep before her shearers and so He opened not His mouth (53:3, 7). Gentleness characterized the life and ministry of Jesus of Nazareth, the suffering Servant of the Lord par excellence. Because He dealt kindly even with His opponents, He could describe Himself as "gentle and humble in heart" (Matt. 11:29). His meekness and gentleness are a model for all Christians to follow (2 Cor. 10:1).

The apostle charged his friend Timothy to strive for right-eousness, godliness, faith, love, endurance, and gentleness. These are linked with Jesus Christ, and they are possible in the life of believers as fruit of the Holy Spirit's work in their hearts (Gal. 5:22–23). Living close to Jesus Christ allows the Spirit to conform believers to the likeness of the Savior, and to adorn their lives with His fruit.

C. Fight (6:12a)

Another challenge to Timothy was to wage a good Christian fight. The command was "fight the good fight of the faith." "Fight" (*agōnizomai*) means to carry on a contest or a war. The term was used for both sporting contests and military conflicts. Both ideas are found in Paul's thought and both may be combined here. In 1 Corinthians 9:24–25 athletic games are in view:

> Do you not know that in a race all the runners run, but only one gets the prize? Run in such a way as to get the prize. Everyone who competes in the games goes into strict training. They do it to get a crown that will not last; but we do it to get a crown that will last forever.

On the other hand, 2 Corinthians 10:3–4 uses the language of military struggle:

> For though we live in the world, we do not wage war as the world does. The weapons we fight with are not the weapons of the world. On the contrary, they have divine power to demolish strongholds.

Whether in athletic competition or in war, the implication of the term *fight* is that it involves great exertion and a disciplined struggle. The words of Paul in Colossians 1:29 make this clear. "To this end I labor, struggling (*agōnizomai*) with all his energy, which so powerfully works in me."

The apostle called Timothy to carry on the holy struggle, "the good [*kalos*, "noble"] fight." This is the noble struggle, the good fight, that Paul could later claim to have completed (2 Tim. 4:7). As a preacher and teacher of the gospel, he encountered many adversaries. The divine message that he proclaimed led him into conflict with carnal men (2 Cor. 7:5) and with "the powers of this dark world . . . the spiritual forces of evil" (Eph. 6:12). Though it involved hardship and suffering, his struggle, his fight, was worthwhile.

What Paul recommended was that Timothy be unrelenting in carrying on that fight. To do that, he would constantly involve himself in the struggle that goes with holding forth the gospel. It would require of him, as it does of all Christians, his best efforts in the strength of Jesus Christ. It would involve him, as it does all who enter this struggle, in labor and in sacrifice.

D. Take (6:12b)

Making still another appeal, the apostle called on Timothy to take hold of the victor's prize, eternal life. This life is a gift from God and is deeply rooted in the resurrection of Christ. Embodying in Himself God's own living power, the Savior conquered death in His resurrection. Aware of that, Paul declared that He "has destroyed death and has brought life and immortality to light through the gospel" (2 Tim. 1:10).

Everlasting life is a future reward. It is life from the dead and beyond the grave, but it can be seized by faith even now. The present possession of eternal life appears to have been Paul's emphasis when he urged Timothy to get a good grip on eternal life.[3] Securing as a present reality the new life in Christ, Timothy was assured of eternal life when the last enemy, death, is vanquished (1 Cor. 15:26, 28). Like Timothy, all Christians are called by God to eternal life. Already "the believer's new life exists." Not yet, however, has this new life been fully manifested. It will not be until that miraculous transformation of the body, when the believer is caught up into the presence of Christ (1 Cor. 15:20ff.; 1 Thess. 4:13–17).

---

3. The force of the aorist imperative (*epilabou*) denotes a single, decisive act. Timothy was not commanded to keep on laying hold of eternal life but to lay hold on that prize in a single act.

II. A Christian's Motivation (6:12c-14)

As he was bringing the letter to a close, the apostle gave to Timothy a fourfold exhortation. (1) "Flee from all this." (2) "Pursue righteousness, godliness, faith, love, endurance and gentleness." (3) "Fight the good fight of the faith." (4) "Take hold of the eternal life." Then he went on to spur Timothy to holiness and service. He stated four reasons why the young man should be faithful to the gospel.

A. Timothy's Vocation (6:12c)

God called Timothy to eternal life. Upon hearing this summons he made a decision to follow Christ. On that occasion he was saved from the penalty of sin, and the Holy Spirit armed him with strength for his new life. The call to eternal and holy life was due to no merit of his own. For as Paul later wrote, "God . . . has saved us and called us to a holy life—not because of anything we have done but because of his own purpose and grace" (2 Tim. 1:9).

B. Timothy's Confession (6:12d-13a)

After Timothy came to faith, he made a good confession in the presence of fellow Christians.[4] The substance of his confession must have been that "Jesus is Lord" and God is the sustainer of all things in life. Such a public confession was an appropriate response to the forgiveness of sins. Timothy acknowledged Jesus Christ as Lord and bore witness that God raised Him from the dead.

Making this kind of confession involves not only an open declaration of Christ's lordship but also a submission to it. The Christian has experienced God's faithfulness in forgiving sins and his confession of Christ as Lord is a mark that he has entered into the new life of faith and is committed to living out his life in obedience to God. When he took the vows of church

---

4. Some scholars associate Timothy's confession with his baptism, but the allusion probably is to the occasion when the elders laid their hands on him (1 Tim. 4:14).

membership, he pledged in the presence of many Christians his faithfulness to the doctrine and teaching of the Scriptures.

C. Timothy's Example (6:13b)

The fortitude of Jesus Christ provided Timothy with the supreme example for the Christian life. Before Pontius Pilate Christ Himself "made the good confession." Under duress He remained faithful and did not falter, even when He knew that His life was in great danger. Indeed Jesus bore a good testimony. When He was asked by Pilate, "Are you the king of the Jews?" He replied, "Yes, it is as you say." Jesus sealed His witness to His kingship with His own life. The fact that Christ stood the test against temptations and fought "the good fight of faith" should inspire the Christian to do likewise. When a Christian suffers for his faith, he can be assured that his Lord also suffered. When a Christian endures adversities, temptations, and sufferings in love and patience, he can be confident that he is walking in his Lord's footsteps. The Lord is his example. The believer makes "the good confession" by remaining loyal in word and deed.

D. Timothy's Look Forward (6:14)

The center of the Christian hope is the second appearance (*epiphaneia,* "manifestation") of Jesus Christ. What He began on His first appearance will be completed at His return. As the Christian's salvation rests on Christ so does his expectation of the fulfillment of all things.

Paul knew the forward look of the believer was a strong incentive for holy living. So he charged Timothy "to keep this commandment without spot or blame until the appearing of our Lord Jesus Christ." The commandment could have been his commission that accompanied the laying on of hands by the elders or even the various admonitions that are stated in the epistle. The real concern was that he maintain the Christian doctrine with which he had been entrusted and that he bring its impact to bear on the lives of men and women.

The second coming of Christ reminded Timothy of the importance of discharging his responsibility "without spot or blame." He was to serve faithfully so that no one could accuse him of slackness and neglect of his work. More important was the judgment of God. Human history is moving toward the day of Christ's second appearing. When this great climax is reached, Timothy and all mankind will have to give an account of their deeds to the sovereign Lord. The day of judgment will be both terrible and glorious. All of life's records will be open. The life and work of each Christian will finally be examined by the Lord. Those who have fought the good fight of faith and have come to long for His appearance will receive on that day a crown of righteousness (2 Tim. 4:8).

III. A Christian's Confidence in God's Uniqueness (6:15-16)

The time of Christ's return is completely in the hands of God. Thinking about God's sovereign control led Paul to celebrate His uniqueness and to launch into a magnificent doxology.

A. God, the One Who Is the Blessed and Only Ruler (6:15b)

This affirms the absolute authority of God. The words "only Ruler, King of kings and Lord of lords" assert the supreme rule of God. He is sovereign over all earthly powers and authority. His authority is not delegated to Him but is fundamental to His own person. His reign knows no limits and no end. He is Lord of every lord, and He is King of every king. The sovereign power of God is celebrated by the apostle John when he exclaims, "Hallelujah! For our Lord God Almighty reigns" (Rev. 19:6). The authority of God is not a threat but a comfort to the Christian. For through Christ the believer is in fellowship with the One who possesses unlimited power.

B. God, the One Who Alone Has Immortality (6:16a)

The sovereign Lord possesses in Himself immortality. Jesus spoke of God the Father as having life in Himself (John 5:26). He is "King eternal, immortal, invisible" (1 Tim. 1:17). He is the One

161

existing before the foundation of the world "from everlasting to everlasting" (Ps. 90:2) and One whose "years will never end" (Ps. 102:27). God is the One "who gives life to everything" (1 Tim. 6:13). No creature has life in itself; all of life is a gift of God. He is the One who bestows the gift of eternal life on individuals.

Human life is characterized by change and mortality, but the immortality of God makes us long for immortality and permanence. This desire can be satisfied. God's immortality and man's mortality were united in Christ Jesus. Christ came into man's mortality and embraced death on behalf of him. In so doing, He "has destroyed death and has brought life and immortality to light through the gospel" (2 Tim. 1:10).

C. God, the One Who Lives in Unapproachable Light (6:16b)

The character of God is described in terms of "light." In Scripture, the term *light* expresses various ideas, such as salvation, knowledge, truth, goodness, and holiness. Of course God is the supreme embodiment of all of these qualities, but the statement that He "lives in unapproachable light" expresses his separateness from all men and creatures. He is infinitely above all things. He is above the universe, high above all of creation. He is not limited to Jerusalem or to the church. Since this is true, it can be said that He lives in light that no one can approach.

God is far off, but He is also near at hand. "He is not far from each one of us. 'For in him we live and move and have our being'" (Acts 17:27b–28). Men find themselves separated from God not because they are finite but because they are sinners. They reject His holy demands and His offers of love and exclude themselves from God and His life-giving power. Due to their sinfulness men have forfeited fellowship with their Creator. But a way of approach has been opened for sinners. God "who lives in unapproachable light" has taken the initiative in reopening the way to fellowship through the gospel. 1 John 1:3b, 7 states so well this tremendous truth: "And our fellowship is with the Father and with his Son, Jesus Christ. . . . But if we walk in the light, as he [God] is in the light, we have fellowship with one another, and the blood of Jesus, his Son, purifies us from every sin."

D. God, the One Whom No One Has Seen (6:16b)

The transcendent, sovereign Lord is hidden from our eyes. God cannot be the object of our sight and never has been seen in His full glory and splendor by man. "No one has seen or can see" Him in the fullness of His majesty. As the Lord told Moses, "man shall not see me and live. . . . and while my glory passes by I will put you in a cleft of the rock, . . . and you shall see my back; but my face shall not be seen" (Exod. 33:20-23, RSV).

God cannot be grasped like any other object in the world. By the use of his own abilities man cannot discover what God is like. Only God Himself can make God known. What is needed is God's revelation of Himself. The supreme revelation of God took a personal form. As John wrote, "No one has ever seen God, but God the only Son, who is at the Father's side, has made him known" (John 1:18). The invisible God became visible in Jesus Christ. God's own nature was revealed in Christ's character, in His mighty works, and in His righteousness and love. As the Word of God, Christ was the supreme manifestation of God. For man to benefit from that saving revelation, he must receive it.

E. God, the One to Whom Be Honor and Might Forever (6:16c)

The supreme authority of God over the whole of creation should lead us to confess His greatness. All honor is due Him. His mighty power is to be celebrated by all of mankind, especially by the redeemed. His gracious care of the world—the provision for rain and sunshine, the cycle of the seasons—remind us not only of His power but also of His bountiful goodness to all people. Behind the world stands God who is good and all-powerful and who has manifested "his incomparably great power for us who believe. That power is like the working of his mighty strength, which he exerted in Christ when he raised him from the dead and seated him at his right hand in the heavenly realms, far above all rule and authority, power and dominion, and every title that can be given, not only in the present age but also in the one to come" (Eph. 1:19–21). He has blessed us "with every spiritual blessing in Christ" (Eph. 1:3). "To him be honor and might forever."

IV. Conclusion

As he advised Timothy, so Paul urges every Christian to "flee" from sin, "pursue" the life that pleases God, "fight the good fight of the faith," and "take" a firm hold on eternal life. To put it another way, the believer is to guard what has been entrusted to his care (1 Tim. 6:20). He is to know what God's Word says and maintain the cardinal doctrines of Scripture.

In these grievous times and in this permissive society evil men and imposters still seek to destroy the foundations of the faith. They promote ways of thinking and living that are at variance with the Word of God. Christians should not be swept from their moorings by secularist influences and by sin and error. They have ample motivation for standing firm in their faith. They are the people of God. They have been called to eternal life and have confessed that Jesus Christ is their Lord. They have Christ as an example to inspire them to faithfulness and the assurance that Christ at His second coming will complete the good work that He has begun in them.

The fact that many Christians are more influenced by secular thinking and culture than by Christian teaching has created a crisis of truth and faith and a crisis of life and morality. The church and every Christian have the responsibility of constantly holding on to and reasserting the basics, such as the sovereignty of the triune God, the deity of Christ, His atoning death, His bodily resurrection, His coming again, the ministry of the Holy Spirit, the divine inspiration of the Scriptures, and biblical teaching on personal integrity and sexual morality.

We must hold to the fundamentals of the faith against all perversions. We must test critically yet humbly the teachings of men in light of the Scriptures. There is no doubt that God Himself preserves the truth of the gospel, but the believer himself must play his part in guarding and maintaining the truth. So we are to keep it pure whatever the cost. We are to guard it against every corruption. We are to remain loyal to it and hand it on to others, for the gospel leads to true life that will be given in its fullness at the coming of Christ.

Bibliography

Arrington, French L. *Paul's Aeon Theology in 1 Corinthians*. Washington, DC: University Press of America, 1977.

Barackman, Paul F. *The Epistles to Timothy and Titus*. Grand Rapids: Baker, 1962.

Barclay, William. *The Letters to Timothy, Titus and Philemon*. Philadelphia: Westminster, 1956.

Barker, Glenn W.; Lane, William L.; and Michaels, J. Ramsey. *The New Testament Speaks*. New York: Harper & Row, 1969.

Barrett, C. K. *The Pastoral Epistles*. The New English Bible. Oxford: Clarendon Press, 1963.

Bauer, Walter. Edited and translated by William F. Arndt and F. Wilbur Gingrich. *A Greek-English Lexicon of the New Testament and Other Early Christian Literature*. Chicago: University of Chicago Press, 1961.

Brown, Colin, ed. *The New International Dictionary of New Testament Theology*. Grand Rapids: Zondervan, 1975–1978.

Cantinat, Jean. *The Epistles of Paul Explained*. Translated by Malachy Carroll. New York: Alba House, 1967.

Dibelius, Martin; and Conzelmann, Hans. *The Pastoral Epistles*. Translated by Philip Buttolph and Adela Yarbro. Philadelphia: Fortress, 1972.

Ellis, E. Earle. *Paul and His Recent Interpreters*. Grand Rapids: Eerdmans, 1961.

Gasque, W. Ward; and Martin, Ralph P., eds. *Apostolic History and the Gospel*. Grand Rapids: Eerdmans, 1970.

Gealy, Fred D.; and Noyes, Morgan P. *The First and Second Epistle to Timothy and the Epistle to Titus*. The Interpreter's Bible. New York: Abingdon, 1955.

Guthrie, Donald. *New Testament Introduction.* Downers Grove, IL: Inter-Varsity, 1970.

———. *New Testament Theology.* Downers Grove, IL: Inter-Varsity, 1981.

———. *The Pastoral Epistles.* Tyndale New Testament Commentaries. Grand Rapids: Eerdmans, 1957.

———. *The Pastoral Epistles and the Mind of Paul.* London: The Tyndale Press, 1956.

Hagner, Donald A.; and Harris, Murray J., eds. *Pauline Studies.* Grand Rapids: Eerdmans, 1980.

Hanna, Robert. *A Grammatical Aid to the Greek New Testament.* Volume 2: *Romans to Revelation.* Hidalgo, Mexico: Instituto Linguistico de Verano, 1980.

Hanson, Anthony T. *The Pastoral Letters.* The Cambridge Bible Commentary. Cambridge: The University Press, 1966.

Higgins, A. J. B. "The Pastoral Epistles." In *Peake's Commentary on the Bible.* Edited by Matthew Black. London: Thomas Nelson and Sons, 1962.

Jensen, Irving L. *1 and 2 Timothy and Titus.* Chicago: Moody, 1973.

Kent, Homer A., Jr. "The Centrality of Scripture." *Journal of the Evangelical Theological Society* 14 (1971): 157–164.

———. *The Pastoral Epistles.* Chicago: Moody, 1958.

Kittel, Gerhard; and Friedrich, Gerhard, eds. *Theological Dictionary of the New Testament.* Translated by G. W. Bromiley. Grand Rapids: Eerdmans, 1964–1976.

Ladd, George E. *A Theology of the New Testament.* Grand Rapids: Eerdmans, 1974.

Lane, William L. "1 Tim. IV. 1–3. An Early Instance of Over-Realized Eschatology?" *New Testament Studies* 11 (January 1965): 164–169.

Lock, Walter. *The Pastoral Epistles.* The International Critical Commentary. Edinburgh: T. & T. Clark, 1924.

Marshall, I. Howard, ed. *New Testament Interpretation.* Grand Rapids: Eerdmans, 1978.

———. "Orthodoxy and Heresy in Earlier Christianity." *Themelios* 2 (1976): 5–14.

Martin, Ralph P. *New Testament Foundations: A Guide for Christian Students.* Volume 2. Grand Rapids: Eerdmans, 1978.

Metzger, Bruce M. "A Reconsideration of Certain Arguments Against the Pauline Authorship of the Pastoral Epistles." *The Expository Times* 70 (1958): 91–94.

Morris, Leon. *I Timothy, II Timothy, Philemon, Hebrews, James.* Understanding the New Testament. London: Scripture Union, 1969.

167

Scott, E. F. *The Pastoral Epistles*. The Moffatt New Testament Commentary. London: Hodder and Stoughton, 1936.

Spencer, Aida Dina Besancon. "Eve at Ephesus." *Journal of the Evangelical Theological Society* 17 (1974): 215–222.

Stott, John R. W. *Guard the Gospel*. Downers Grove, IL: Inter-Varsity, 1973.

White, Newport J. D. "The First and Second Epistles to Timothy and the Epistle to Titus." In *The Expositor's Greek Testament*. Grand Rapids: Eerdmans, n.d.

Yamauchi, Edwin. *Pre-Christian Gnosticism*. Grand Rapids: Eerdmans, 1973.